Real Estate: Play the Game Like the Winners

The major keys to making 6 figures in Real Estate and using it to create generational wealth

Casanova Brooks

Table of Contents

Introduction 3

Chapter 1: Why Real Estate? - 5 Practical Success Stories 12

Chapter 2: The Mindset to Start in Real Estate 20

Chapter 3: Lead Generation is the Key 42

Chapter 4: Discipline Wins Championships 55

Chapter 5: Real Estate is a Contact Sport 63

Chapter 6: 5 Star Presentations 71

Chapter 7: Act Like You've Done it Before 88

Chapter 8: Promoting Your Real Estate Business Online 104

Chapter 9: Creating Passive Income is the Key 126

Chapter 10: The Life of a Small Business Owner 136

Chapter 11: Time is our Most Valuable Asset 142

Chapter 12: 4x Your Life 147

Conclusion 150

Introduction

I want to thank you and congratulate you for choosing to read my book, *"Real Estate: Play the game like winners"*.

My purpose for writing this book is to share the tactical tips and tricks I've used to build my real estate empire, with new and even seasoned agents and to teach agents the powers that lie within the industry of helping clients to sell, buy, or even invest in real estate. While much of the advice I'll share over the course of this book will be considered advice for real estate agents, I would agree to say it can also be adapted over any form of sales and industry. The reason being is because real estate, like any other product-based industry, isn't based on the success of the product but the relationships and service displayed to get to the closing table. That's where the shift in mindset comes in. A shift from transactional to relationship-based, since, after all, we're not in the home selling business but the **people business**.

My Story

When I got into real estate, I didn't have a clue how to sell real estate, let alone run a business. I had to figure it out quickly though, as I could see the little savings my family had in our bank account start to dwindle away. Excuses weren't going to keep a roof over my families' head and so I had to implement a shift in my mindset. From a young age, I never had a blueprint on how to be successful, I always did it my way. Not this time though, I knew this time had to be different.

In this book, I focus on sharing exactly how I managed to make six figures in my first full year in real estate in a new city with no sphere, previous clients, or background in the field. I'll share the tactical and practical tips I learned and how I developed the mindset to not use my challenges as a crutch, but to see them as an opportunity to do something no one who looked like me, or had a background like mine, had done before.

Before I got into real estate, I had many different jobs, from playing online poker for a living for 2 years, being a repo manager at Rent-A-Center, working in a call center servicing Vizio customers, selling cars, and even a marketing consultant selling yellow pages in a digital era. That's just to name some of the more prominent jobs. My point is, I tried it all. I had success in them all as well, and while I had bigger success over others, I always knew there was something bigger out there for me.

I read a book in the early stages of my sales career by the great Robert Kiyosaki called *Rich dad poor dad.* That book changed my life but what really stuck out for me was that I was trading time for money. The only way I could earn money was by letting someone else control my time, which always made me uneasy. That's where real estate came in. When I first decided to get into real estate, I heard a phrase that will forever stick with me, "*he (or she) who owns the land makes the rules.*" I thought that if I could get into real estate and start to own land, no one would control my time and it would allow me to have the freedom to build a life by design, that I never needed a vacation from. When I first reflected on my life at the time I first heard that saying, I knew at that very moment, if I wanted to create wealth for my family and, most importantly, get more of my time back, I needed to invest in and own some real estate. The only challenge in front of me was looking back on my past and upbringing, from being raised in inner city south side of Chicago to being moved and finishing out my teen years in Sioux City, Iowa... my parents never owned a home, car, business, or anything else that could generate wealth or a passive income. So, how was I supposed to know how to create a life like this when no one else around me had ever done it?

Like many, growing up in poverty-stricken neighborhoods, I was exposed to the fast life at a young age. You know, gambling, gangs, guns, and selling drugs. I was fortunate enough though that most of the older guys around, who were involved in the lifestyle, had a lot of respect for my mom. They tried to distance from me as much as possible and I never got into any trouble. Early on, I remember always being fascinated by the wealthiest people on Forbes list. People like Richard Branson, Mark Cuban, Tony Robbins, and even Jay-Z and P. Diddy owned some type of big yacht or mansions that I would daydream and envision myself one day owning. I didn't know what I could do to get this type of wealth, but I always had big dreams and a strong urge to succeed in life so that I could afford some of the finer things. Again, my only issue was that I didn't have the slightest clue or blueprint as to how I would make it happen (legally).

Advantages I Had-

One advantage I was fortunate enough to have working in my favor was being born in the late 80s and being raised through the age of digital era. Because of the Internet, combined with the likes of Google and YouTube, I kept finding that the information was out there. I just had to be willing to put in a little extra effort and go seek it out. As the saying goes, *"I knew that if it was meant to be...It was up to me."*

In my mind, I always used to think that the richest people must never have to go to work and just get paid to watch others work. How wrong I was though! I read a lot of articles and books about how the wealthiest Americans accumulate their wealth. At that time, I discovered a common denominator for 90% of them that was key in helping them build, maintain, and grow their wealth. The majority of them were real estate owners and investors. Later on in life, this realization would become a major key in helping develop my mindset shift and give clarity about the field I knew I eventually wanted to end up in...REAL ESTATE.

Growing up in the inner city, my mom and I always lived in rental houses and apartments. The mindset was that as long as we had a roof over our heads, that's all that mattered. In many ways, I totally agreed with this mindset but there was never any talk of saving money at all, let alone saving for down payments on a home or building credit to acquire rental properties for our own legacy. It was, and in many cases, still is a backwards mentality that plagues our culture as a whole. That mindset of constantly working for money instead of finding ways to make money work for them.

All their paychecks would go to buying Jordan's, cars, Gucci clothes, Michael Kors, renting houses, etc. All these depreciating items only set us back mentally. It made them feel like they were winning, when in reality, they were digging deeper into a hole. That constant rat race was going on not only in the workplace, but in our homes as well. My mom always used to let me know that she was, *"robbing Peter to pay Paul"* in order to give me anything she could. The biggest problem with that was, she never found ways to pay herself so that she no longer needed to rob Peter. So, I knew that for me to have something different in life, I had to find ways to **"own"** so others could pay me.

How Other People Are Successful?

I had read many stories about how people who were very successful in their fields had used real estate to build their long-term passive wealth. I specifically remember reading an anecdote about Roger Staubach. Known by NFL fans as *"Captain Comeback"* in his days, Roger was the second-highest rated passer of all time. He was also an MVP Winner and Super Bowl champion in the NFL. Despite his immense success in the NFL, Roger didn't make his millions from football...but from real estate. He retired and started The Staubach Company, a real estate firm that helped clients find offices, retail and industrial spaces. The company grew to 50 field offices in North America and was worth $640 million dollars by the time it was sold to Jones Lang LaSalle in 2008.

Ellen DeGeneres, the comedian and TV host, is another example in the public limelight of how playing the real estate game could contribute to wealth. DeGeneres and actress, Portia De Rossi, purchased the nearly $40 million **Brody House** in Los Angeles and later sold it for a whopping profit of $15 million!

It was clear to me that people were making some serious money by owning real estate. The only problem I was faced with, was that I had no blueprint as to how to make it happen for me. How could I get to a destination that there were no roadmaps for? Hunger & Persistence. I always believed if I just kept trying to figure out my purpose and never accepting no for an answer, I would eventually find my way. My first step was to make sure no one would belittle my spirit and dreams, and the thought of owning any type of real estate fueled my soul. Have you ever observed an infant growing into the toddler stage? Did you notice how many times they get told "no", yet they still persist and seem to get their way in the end? It's because they've made up their mind that they're going to be victorious in the end.

Early on, most of what I learned about real estate came from reading articles and checking people out on Forbes. Real estate seemed to pop up every time I clicked a name in the Forbes list. It had been the third-largest source of wealth among the ultra-rich, with 163 billionaires. Real estate helped create 8 out of the top 10 wealthiest. Even though they may not have gotten their start in real estate, they owned a significant portion which served as a catalyst for driving their wealth from the beginning. After reading many of their stories, it seemed just like monopoly (my favorite game growing up). In my mind, I just needed to own a bunch of property so when people landed on it (or needed the space for anything they wanted), they would have to pay up. Even better, if someone needed to sell for any reason, I had the capital and power to buy it from them and grow more wealth while building my portfolio. Now, of course, it's a little different in the real world as there's insurance and taxes you'll have to pay to Uncle Sam, but that can be taken care of by someone landing on your property (or paying your rent). Owning must always be the end goal.

You could be starting the process of getting your license, or have a few years of experience in the business. You may be a seasoned veteran looking to grow to the next level, or just someone thinking of owning some real estate and making money...this book will teach you what myself and many other successful real estate hustlers have done to be consistently successful.

How this book is different from every other real estate book out there

1. Radical transparency... The information and tips you will learn from this book have been proven over time by any successful agent you can think of. I learned and used each of these to grow my business from 0 clients and no sphere of influence in my community, to doing 46 transactions worth 8 million dollars in volume in my first year in real estate.

2. I was also awarded as rookie of the year in my city. The methods won't be rocket science, but there will be a lot of 'aha' moments throughout and if you are disciplined enough to make sure you perform these tactical and practical tips... you will be able to accomplish whatever goals you have: simply combine it with discipline and hustle. If you focus on adapting the mindset we're going to go over in this book, along with the tactical strategies, there's no way you won't hit the ground running and ultimately succeed in real estate. They say discipline is the bridge between goals and accomplishment: I definitely believe that. The reason most agents aren't as successful as they want to be is because they lack the discipline to do the little things that count. Hopefully, after reading this book, you'll be able to identify those things and get a jumpstart wherever you are in your career. What you'll notice is that this book will be a bridge into the mind of a realtor that understands there's more to the business than just helping

others buy and sell real estate. Also, owning real estate for yourself to create *"mailbox money"*! If you're not sure what mailbox money is, don't worry, we'll dive into that later in the book. For now, let's work on navigating the business to create steady commission checks so you can ultimately buy the real estate!

Thanks again for grabbing this book, I hope you enjoy it!

© **Copyright 2018 by <u>Casanova Brooks</u> - All rights reserved.**

This document is geared towards providing exact and reliable information in regards to the topic and issue covered. The publication is sold with the idea that the publisher is not required to render accounting, officially permitted, or otherwise, qualified services. If advice is necessary, legal or professional, a practiced individual in the profession should be ordered.

- From a Declaration of Principles which was accepted and approved equally by a Committee of the American Bar Association and a Committee of Publishers and Associations. In no way is it legal to reproduce, duplicate, or transmit any part of this document in either electronic means or in printed format. Recording of this publication is strictly prohibited and any storage of this document is not allowed unless with written permission from the publisher. All rights reserved.

The information provided herein is stated to be truthful and consistent, in that any liability, in terms of inattention or otherwise, by any usage or abuse of any policies, processes, or directions contained within is the solitary and utter responsibility of the recipient reader. Under no circumstances will any legal responsibility or blame be held against the publisher for any reparation, damages, or monetary loss due to the information herein, either directly or indirectly.The respective author owns all copyrights not held by the publisher. The information herein is offered for informational purposes solely and is universal. The presentation of the information is without contract or any type of guarantee assurance.

The trademarks that are used are without any consent, and the publication of the trademark is without permission or backing by the trademark owner. All trademarks and brands within this book are for clarifying purposes only and are owned by the owners themselves, not affiliated with this document.

Chapter 1:

Why Real Estate? - 5 Practical Success Stories

Getting started in real estate can be a huge fear for anyone. I say getting started because many never even overcome the fear of not passing the exam. I can't tell you how many people have reached out about getting their license, only to talk to me months later and they're still in the same boat. Most people are held back by that fear and doubt. The fear of not passing the test, losing money and savings, the fear of failure, the fear of the unknown, and, hell, even the fear of becoming truly successful. The beauty of it though, if you're willing to go all in and you want the success, is that you can find it. Many people have won in real estate and created the life of their dreams. I'll share a few practical success stories that you might already be familiar with.

Barbara Corcoran

You may not recognize the name Barbara Corcoran but I'm sure you've seen her before. She's a shark tank investor and is becoming a household name in America, all thanks to her pursuits in real estate. Over a period of a few decades, Barbara was able to turn a $1,000 loan into a $70 million empire.

Before she ventured into real estate, Barbara said she worked 22 different jobs. She was fed up taking orders and didn't want to work for anyone else. With near- zero experience, she obtained a $1,000 loan from her then boyfriend, and set out to find success of her own. A few decades later, in 2001, Barbara sold her brokerage - The Corcoran Group - for $66 million.

Barbara says that hiring resilient people is one secret that helped her find success in real estate. She learned to spot people who were most likely to succeed, even if they had no prior experience, and make them a part of her business. During interviews, she looked for people who had overcome obstacles in the past and who saw failure as a challenge to succeed. Barbara also says that when she got her first check, she didn't spend it on food, rent, or other necessities. She went straight to Bergdorf Goodman and purchased a very expensive coat. "If I looked like I was capable, then I was capable," she says. Barbara has been an expert at creating the illusion of popularity. She was able to create excellent media reports on real estate market trends, despite the fact that her own crawling business had low sales. Before long, she was being quoted by the New York Times as a real estate expert, giving the impression that her firm was much bigger (and more successful) than it actually was. This gave her the advantage to build her brand faster.

Barbara says that "everybody wants what everybody wants". At one time, she asked her sales people to invite their best clients to a secret sale (where the prices would be revealed on the specified day). More than 200 people showed up to look at 88 properties. Many of these bought less than ideal apartments just because they saw 100 more people who wanted them too. Barbara reinforces that everyone should know they have the right to succeed. She learned to acknowledge that she could succeed when she was still a little-known player in the New York real estate scene. Doing this gave her the confidence she needed to follow the ambitious path, even when conditions were not favorable.

In addition to her success in real estate, Barbara is a successful entrepreneur in many ways. She is regularly appearing on national TV, charging over $70,000 for speaking gigs, and invests in many different companies. Her story should serve as an inspiration to anyone who's looking to get their real estate ambitions off the ground.

Jay Morrison

Popularly known as "Mr. Real Estate", Jay Morrison is an inspiring real estate success story. Despite being a high school dropout, at-risk youth, and a three-time felon, Jay was able to make major life transformations and succeed in many areas. Jay is the perfect example of an incarcerated drug dealer who went from the street corner to the corner office. His success shows that with the right mindset and determination, we can all make it in real estate and other areas of life.

Jay was baptized in the drug trade in the 1980s while growing up in central New Jersey. "My grandmother sold drugs, my father sold drugs, my mom sold drugs, and I grew up to sell drugs," he says. Like many other black youths caught up in the drug business, he led a dangerous lifestyle and spent time in prison on more than one occasion. While in jail, he would work 8-hour shifts mopping floors and picking up trash – and earning 13 cents a day. It put a different perspective on life and freedom as he knew it and may have ignited the sparks that eventually compelled him to change. Morrison started questioning the direction his life was taking in his mid-20s. He says that he could see himself either dead or in jail by the time he turned 30. That's when he decided on a paradigm shift. He broke his burner (drug-dealing cell phone), offloaded his work to a partner, and dived into real estate. Morrison started by working for a mortgage company while on parole for drug offences. He familiarized himself with real estate and took about a year to learn as much as he needed about the real estate business, as well as develop a professional etiquette and culture. He used people skills that he learned during his drug dealing days to build a clientele and brought total honesty to all his interactions. With hard work and dedication, he was able to work his way up to being a real estate owner and the "lord of his land".

Mr. Morrison published his first book "Hip Hop 2 Homeowners: How WE Build Wealth in America" in response to Hip Hop trends that he felt were hurting the community by encouraging wasteful spending and a drug culture. The book allowed people to get into his mind and understand what he was trying to do for the culture. Today, Jay Morrison has made a name with high-profile athletes, entertainers, and high-profile executives. He is an icon of real estate success, especially for African American youths and has

open up the TREF (Tulsa Real Estate Fund) a real estate crowd fund that allows both credited and non-credited investors to collectively invest and own real estate projects that are unique, diversified, and yield a reasonable rate of return.

Josh Altman

Josh Altman is a classic rags-to-riches story in real estate. Born and bred in Massachusetts, he arrived in LA 13 years ago with no money and started flipping houses while working in a mailroom. At the age of 26, he was a millionaire – only to lose everything 6 months later due to the economic crisis.

Finding success – going back to zero – and being able to bounce back, is what makes this one of my best reference stories for real estate success. Josh Altman shows us that it's not about what happens to you, but rather how you bounce back up from failure.

Today, Mr. Altman is one of the most successful real estate agents in the country. He specializes in the high-end real estate market and sold a cumulative $1.5 billion in real estate between 2013 and 2016. A self-confessed workaholic, Josh says that the more you do your homework, the more likely you are to achieve your real estate goals. He believes that in the real estate game, it doesn't matter who you are – because the principles involved in buying and selling homes are the same for everyone.

What's amazing about this realtor is that he was able to go back to the industry and find success after losing nearly everything in the housing crash. "I knew if I could do it before, I could do it again," he says. Josh was able to take notes from his past mistakes (buying a $500,000 property with essentially no money down) and rebuilt his empire based on solid investment principles.

Mr. Altman credits his success to knowing his products very well. He says he likes to hold onto property for as long as he can. He reads constantly, works hard, and is always on the ground picking up what's happening. Josh Altman has also cultivated a killer negotiation skill set. So, it's no surprise that he was ranked the best luxury realtor in the LA market.

Josh Altman inspires real estate agents to learn the industry, the people, and the properties like the back of their hands. That is what breeds the confidence you need to hook clients to the right property, and essentially make deals happen. Having a dream team is another major success factor from Josh Altman. While rebuilding his real estate empire from the dust after the housing crash, Mr. Altman says that he focused on building strong, authentic relationships with people across the industry. He also put together a trusted team of assistants, which included his now fiancée. Today, Josh Altman is a star in Bravo's "Million Dollar Listing Los Angeles". At the age of 37 years, he is worth over $10 million.

Ryan Serhant

You've probably seen Ryan Serhant on the hit TV show Million Dollar Listing New York. He's been named one of the most influential real estate agents and worked with many of celebrities and wealthy philanthropists. His success was anything but spoon-fed though. Ryan credits himself as a young shy and weird kid growing up. He moved to real estate in 2006 to be an actor. Serhant struggled as an actor and eventually even took anything from bartending jobs and serving to tables and hand modeling gigs. Anything to pay the rent in New York City.

Ryan decided to start as a real estate agent in 2008, during the dark times of the financial crisis. Serhant struggled in his first year in real estate, only making $9,000. Despite the rather slow start, he knew that he had the drive and endurance to succeed in the real estate space since he had struggled to make ends meet before. Serhant said that failing in his acting career taught him how to be fearless and overcome objections. Ryan quickly rose to the top of the game in New York City. Within his first two years as a licensed realtor, he sold 100-million dollars' worth of real estate By 2012, he was ranched #15 of the 100 most successful sales people in New York. Around this time is when he also landed the spot on MDLNY. Fast forward ten years later, Real Trends (Real Estate ranking magazine) has Serhant and his team as the top real-estate team for sales volume in NY and #2 in the country.

In 2017 alone, they closed over $835 million worth of real estate property transactions.

What Ryan credits most to being successful so quickly was his mindset. He said, "they would ask me, like, "Who's the best real-estate agent?" And my answer literally was, "You're looking at him." Not necessarily true, but also not untrue. Like I can believe that I'm the best, and no one — who's going to tell me something else? It's really going to come down to kind of the way I portray myself, right? if I scream my own success from a mountaintop, people will hear it, and that's how you'll build your persona, your personality, your career that way."

Grant Cardone

Mr. Cardone (Uncle G as I like to call him) is an internationally-renowned sales trainer, but most of his wealth has been built in real estate. Through his company, Cardone Capital, Grant has moved over $725 million worth of real estate. His company holds multi-millions of dollars' worth of multifamily properties across the country. Grant Cardone is a truly inspiring example of real estate investing success.

His accomplishment serves to show that even when you start with nothing, you have the potential to accumulate wealth and build an empire in this high-potential industry.

Cardone started learning about the real estate business when he was as young as 15 years. After graduating from college, he spent time trying to acquire as much practical knowledge about buying property and other kinds of real estate dealings. At the age of 29, he was finally ready to put his 14 years of real estate knowledge to the test. He had saved enough to buy a single-family home in Houston, which didn't do too well because tenants left after a few months. He quickly sold it and decided to strategize a game plan on how to grow his wealth empire.

Following this dismal performance, Grant shelved his real estate ambitions, but continued to increase his knowledge. Five years later, he bought a 38-unit multi- family complex in San Diego that was worth $1.9 million by making a down payment of $350,000. He acquired a second complex a few months later. In 2012, Grant's company acquired what was referred to as Florida's largest private party acquisition of multifamily real estate for $59 million. This was a portfolio of over 1,000 apartments spread over 5 apartment communities. Through the years, he has been able to amass a $866 portfolio of multi-family real estate. His success journey shows how anyone can use various forms of financing to accumulate wealth through real estate investment.

I decided to tell you the stories about all of these individuals because they all had to overcome many obstacles while taking a risk on an industry they weren't too familiar with in the beginning. They inspired me early on when I first started my journey. They showed me it what was possible. Now maybe you're in a similar situation and you're wondering if you can change your life through real estate. Well I'm here to tell you…you can. No matter if you're currently a banker, teacher, construction worker, self- employed, or even unemployed, today, you have an opportunity to change your future for the better, but the first step is changing your mindset.

Chapter 2:

The Mindset to Start in Real Estate

We've all heard the saying, "Money doesn't grow on trees" probably by our parents when we were kids, and while that's correct, it may grow out of the ground. That's the beauty of real estate. Look around you. No matter what city, state, or country you're in, you can see houses, business buildings, malls, and apartment complexes. All these are investments that make their owners very rich and wealthy over time. Real estate is all around us. It's a crucial part of any economy and there's a lot of potential for people who venture into this industry and are willing to put in the hard work and dedication it takes, not just to succeed over the long-term, but hit the ground running. Be it as agents, developers, or investors, as long as people are buying homes, selling homes, owning businesses, and looking for more passive income, there will always be opportunities around.

I truly believe that, with hard work and consistency, anyone can learn anything. It isn't just about whether you have the natural abilities. Some of the most successful people in real estate started from the unlikeliest of fields. That's because there's no magical talent needed to create success in real estate. Even if you tried to rely solely on your natural abilities to succeed in real estate, just like with anything else in life...it'll only take you so far. No matter how gifted as a smooth talker or negotiator you might be, if you don't consistently prospect, follow up, and market yourself, you'll become obsolete. The bigger question is what will you do to break through once you've achieved some success and have hit your first wall? How would you preserve and achieve your next level of success? In my opinion, the way to break through is having a strong circle, as well as knowing where to get mentorship from others who have already been there and done that. The nugget is in that knowledge.

You are probably already familiar with the saying, "*knowledge is power*", but there's a little more to it than that. See, knowledge is power, but without application of the knowledge, it's useless. It's just like prayers without action. They're just that, prayers. Think of it this way, if you know something (knowledge), then you are only informed. It's like having a recipe. You have to apply the recipe and cook (take action) so you can get the results (ready food). Some real estate agents have a constant need to consume more information – maybe because they feel like they don't know enough to take action. But successful people gather knowledge and direct it to an already DEFINITE purpose. They know that the potential of knowledge can only be realized when it is directed to a definite end result, using practical plans of action.

The 3 Major keys:

"*By failing to prepare, you are preparing to fail.*" - Benjamin Franklin

In this game, it's easy to fall into the trap of staying busy. I say trap because I learned that being busy and actually being productive are two different things. If you spend your days being "busy" but not "productive", then, aftersome success, you're going to burn out Busy realtors jump at every task, productive realtors know how to prioritize what's important and what's urgent. Busy realtors do all their own showings, paperwork, marketing, put up signs and lockboxes, and even show homes way outside of their expertise demographic. Productive realtors understand the real power is in leveraging. Finding and utilizing others on their team that are smarter than them and more efficient in the areas they are not. Productive agents also understand how to decipher what's important and what's urgent. Not everything needs to be done the moment it pops up on your desk. If you were to ask anyone who's spent 5 years or more in real estate, they can tell you that even though it might seem urgent in the moment, very, very few things in real estate need IMMEDIATE action. Your focus should always be prioritizing and taking care of the things that are urgent: this will help all the other tasks fall into place.

How to Start Your Day?

The goal is to start your day with a game plan. No matter how small or simple that may be, this is where so many agents burn out. They run from showing to showing, picking up kids in between, PTA meetings, stopping by the office to do paperwork, sporting events, and emails to end the evening. All just to wake up and repeat the next day. This is a busy agent. The focus has to be on being strategic with your time and finding a way to leverage others around so you're not feeling like you must do it all. After all, time (not money) is the most valuable asset we have in our lives. Most realtor's make the mistake of feeling like they have to do it all. I was fortunate early in my career to learn a phrase a great agent/coach said to me that continues to stick with me, "if you don't have an assistant, you ARE the assistant."

With so many apps and programs out nowadays, you can definitely find tools to help you with the planning and organizing of your day so you're not running around without merit and purpose.

Follow the Pareto Principle

Ever heard of the law of the vital few (also known as the 80/20 rule)? One day in Italy, an economist and scholar named Vilfredo Pareto was spending time in his garden. He noticed that 20% of the pea plants in his garden generated 80% of the healthy pea pods during harvesting. Baffled by this interesting finding, Mr. Pareto applied it to his economics work and was even more thrilled when he realized that 20% of the people in Italy owned roughly 80% of the land. He went on to try the rule in different industries and found it to be consistently true. That's the origin of the 80/20 principle, which states that 80% of results will come from just 20% of the action.

Today, this Pareto principle has been applied in economics, science, software development, sports, occupational health, and other areas with impressive accuracy. It also applies to real estate. Most people are of the notion that direct input of time and effort will deliver results. That may be true, but the Pareto rule tells us that it matters where the time and effort are put. What really matters is, are they in the 80% or the 20%?

When you focus on the 80% that doesn't matter, you'll only get 20% of the results you want, and vice versa. It's clear that whenever we don't focus on doing what matters, we miss out on the results we want. I bet this theory is true for most aspects of our lives. In real estate marketing and sales, you must learn to focus on the 20% that truly counts, so you can get 80% of the results you want.

Below are 3 major components in real estate that are a part of the 20%: so you can put your energy where it really matters.

1. Lead-Generation keeps your business afloat

Real estate is a practical field. It's dominated by the 20% who are movers and shakers and ultimately do 80% of the business. So, how do you become a part of the 20%? Well, first, let me tell you, it doesn't matter whether you're a professor in economics and this is your side gig until you build up enough income to quit or you're a graduate fresh out of college. In this field, it's all about building relationships. If you can't build relationships, attract and cultivate with clients, just like any other small business...you're going to struggle to maintain a successful and sustainable organization. The first step in your daily activities must be lead generation. Without keeping your pipeline full, there is no business. The beauty of real estate is that everyone is a potential client. NAR (The National Association of Real Estate) says 70% of consumers forget their realtor's name after the first year! That's crazy! What that means for the great agents is that, every day, more and more consumers will hit the market without an agent and that means OPPORTUNITY.

Everyone needs a place to live and most would love to be the lord of their land. Even if they already own a home and aren't looking to sell or invest in more real estate...no worries, continue to nurture that relationship as they probably can refer you to someone who is looking to buy, sell, or invest. No one can do business with you if 1.) they don't know you and 2.) they don't know what you do. You can't be a secret agent. If you think about it, this doesn't just apply to real estate agents. It applies to almost anyone in the service industry. The best dentists, cosmetic surgeons, and lawyers need to attract leads so they can make money. Real estate agents, lawyers, doctors, and entrepreneurs...we're all in the lead-generation business. You can't just sit back and hope the work will find you. Knowing how to attract clients is a major ingredient for success. You might be good at talking to people and negotiating deals, but if you're not good at generating leads, then you have a major problem.

To create a business that gives you the kind of income you are targeting, you need to keep the pipeline full. I have met a lot of agents who work really hard but inject their energy into activities that are in the 80% (rather than the 20% that counts). The sooner you embrace the fact that it's the number of QUALIFIED LEADS you have that will grow your business, the better off you will be. Nothing else in your business is going to have more impact than the number of qualified leads you have.

In a thriving market, many agents rely on passive lead generators such as casual referrals, luck, and the occasional networking. But these kinds of agents are most likely to face hardships when the market shifts. There's always a buyer somewhere who has the money and is willing to pay to buy a house. The challenge for real estate agents is to find who this buyer is and where they are. That's where lead generation comes in. By pouring your energy into direct prospecting such as door knocking, cold calling, direct mail, and social media marketing, you'll be doing your best to create business regardless of how the market is doing. I often say to other agents that lead generation is a constant effort. It's like aiming for the Gold medal in the Olympics. You've got to consistently practice and work towards this objective. You can't put it on hold or turn it on and off. You've got to keep doing it. Even when you have more business than you think you can handle, you should never press 'Pause' on your lead generation activities. I learned early on from my broker, Vince Leisey, "*the prospecting we do today is for 30, 60, even 90 days on out.*" You're better off complaining about having too many leads than having none.

To truly be a successful agent and make the type of income you dream of, you must prospect daily, generate leads – and become disciplined enough to not quit prospecting when you're comfortable with the business you're getting.

2. The Golden Nugget is in The Follow-Up

Just like prospecting, consistency is key. Running a real-estate business without proper follow-up is like trying to fetch sand with a tennis racket. It's going to get through the holes and get back where it came from. However good your lead generation is, you risk running a failing real estate business if you don't have a solid follow-up strategy. I learned early on that for real estate agents, follow-up is one of the most effective strategies to win more business. And yet, most agents do not take the time to do it! A study by Marketing Donut shows that 80% of sales require 5 follow-up phone calls after the initial meeting. Nearly half of sales people give up after the first follow-up attempt or, even worse, they build enough report with the potential prospects, gain their contact information, and then never follow-up at all! That's crazy to me. My first ever sale came because of a follow-up. A young couple (who are both still good friends of mine now) came through my new construction open house looking to find a new home before they signed on the dotted line to build custom and wait 8-10 months. Because of how young they looked, and the fact I was still brand new in the business (and hadn't done one deal before), I wasn't too sure whether they were just out strolling through the neighborhood or really looking to pull the trigger soon. Regardless, I chose not to judge and treated them with the utmost respect and attention. I built quick rapport and even suggested I had a great mortgage loan officer I could connect them with to help get pre-approved for their loan. After talking for about 20 minutes, they agreed to put their contact information on the sign-in sheet and allowed me to follow up with them. Not even 2 hours after that open house ended, I followed up via email, thanking them for their time and delivered on my promise by sending over the contact of one of my preferred lenders. Coincidently, Mr. buyer had a home a couple years back that he sold, but before selling, he did a refinance and it was the exact same lender who helped him before! This, in turn, all worked out in my favor and helped me close on my first client and guess what? They bought a $400,000 home with me within the next 30 days! It all started with the follow-up though. You have to think about what steps you can take to master the follow-up process, so you can make sure that you're capitalizing on all your leads.

Proper follow-up is all about communication, nurturing, and being consistent while at it. Create time to call or email contacts you meet during an open house, listing presentation, or any other lead generation activity. Even after you have completed a transaction and the transactions are closed, you still have work to do. Just like lead generation, following up ought to be a consistent, never-ending process. You may want to provide a client with a thank you note, a bottle of champagne, or even a booklet of vouchers for local businesses or seasonal events going on in your local community. It's all about making a small gesture to remind your clients that you're still their agent and you haven't forgotten about them. You should do this over and over again. Remember, out of sight, out of mind.

The national association of realtors published a survey that said 89% of buyers claim they would use their agent a second time around, the problem is, it's also reported that 70% of buyers forget their agent's name after the first year of buying a home. Don't be that agent.

There are innumerable communication options available to help you stay on top of mind:

- ☐ Stay active on social media and keep offering valuable information (show upcoming listings, open houses, etc.).
- ☐ Send regular email newsletters using a CRM or 3rd party program such as MailChimp or constant contact.
- ☐ Send physical mail with end of season wraps, end of year wrap, or local market updates and new events going on.
- ☐ Send text messages to your clients on the anniversary of their purchase date, birthdays, celebration moments, and holidays.
- ☐ Pick up the phone once a quarter just to touch base and check your prospects out (you can also make conversation based off the content your clients have been putting out on social media).
- ☐ Offer a free CMA (property analysis) to show potential sellers how they sit in the market.

Savvy agents will personalize their follow-up communication. If you have been introduced to a referral lead or have made a new contact during a marketing event, you don't want to jump right in and show off your greatest sales results. Focus on connecting with them, listen to their needs, and let them know how you can help them. You may want to find what their real estate goals are, connect on social media, or supply them with valuable information. Cultivate the relationship so they can think of you as THEIR agent and go-to person for all things real estate even if they've worked with another agent in the past.

Are you afraid of seeming too pushy? It's not a secret that a lot of real estate agents put following up aside simply because they're afraid to be too pushy. Well, you're not wrong. That can happen too. However, by analyzing your clients right you can know if your follow up is going to annoy a certain client or not. Some people simply need their space for a bit until they can make a decision. Some actually do need a reminder, a slight nudge. I have a couple of tips that can help with this fear.

First of all, try not to follow up on Monday mornings: people need some time to get back to reality, put their brain and their mind in a working mood and prepare emotionally for the week ahead. If you do your follow up cheerful call on a Monday morning you will definitely run into the risk of pushing your client away. Just pick another day, or at least wait until they're back from lunch.

Another tip of mine is offering something in return with following up. Look, you're obviously asking something from your client when you call or text to see where they're at on the whole buying or selling process. So simply ask yourself, why should they take the time to talk to you? If you offer some value in return you won't get rejected, and you definitely won't annoy them. It can be anything: some new data on the house they're interested in, brochures from a reliable bank that will lend them the loan, etc.

And lastly, try to give them some good energy when following up. Put yourself in their shoes and hear yourself following up. If it sounds depressing and not at all exciting, that you have to change something. Maybe it's the tone of your voice, since you're feeling down today, which, by the way, should never reflect your work. Maybe it's the words you use: change them up a bit, make sure you sound authentic but also upbeat. And most importantly, don't forget to be nice: hello, how are you, thank you for your time, I appreciate it. Just some words that might make or break your deal.

3.) Know the numbers

When I first got my license, I had very little savings so I was still trying to work another job to cover me until I could replace my w2 income. The problem was, in real estate, your income is a direct result of the time you've put in. If you're working part-time, you're most likely going to be receiving part-time income. I knew I needed to go all in but the problem was that I wasn't sure how to calculate how much money I needed to be able to 1.) replace my income or 2.) live the lifestyle I wanted. These were the things no one teaches you. I knew it would be tough to get to my end destination if I didn't at least map out a plan to get there. How successful do you think you would be if every moment of the day you were thinking about the money you didn't have? It's hard to focus on doing what you need to focus on for the long-term (daily prospecting) when you're constantly looking at the short-term (your bank account today). That's why knowing your numbers inside and out is critical. Some of the metrics that are very important to track are:

- Business expenses (marketing, office fees, MLS fees, gas, E&O insurance)
- Lead generation services you're investing in (Zillow, Realtor.com, CRM, MailChimp, Direct Mail, etc.)

These are all things that can add up monthly. If they are not accounted for in the beginning once the commission checks come rolling in, especially if you've depleted your savings to take the jump into real estate. you'll be chasing your tail and playing the same game of the rat race, living paycheck to paycheck. Even when your commission checks come in, there's broker splits, government taxes, and more, that should be calculated for before that deal is closed. My advice is to always put 30-35% (everyone's number is different) aside into a separate bank account. This way you're not worried about being short on what Uncle Sam is looking for.

Busting the Myths

The only thing that's keeping you from getting what you want is the stories you keep telling yourself. - Tony Robbins

Myths are sewn into us at an early age and they lead to fears that hold us back. Our basic beliefs are fundamental to success in the real estate industry. Before we can achieve the highest levels of success, we must be able to tackle our core beliefs about success. However real or unreal they are, they may impact our chances at success. The good thing about fears and myths is that they can be educated out just as they were educated in.

In the bible for realtors, '*The Millionaire Real Estate Agent*", author Gary Keller, highlights the most common myths that hold real estate agents back. You need to bust these myths in order to achieve your full potential.

Myth #1 – "I could never do that"

First, let me ask you...Is anyone ever fully aware of their end potential? Do we ever truly know up front what we can achieve? I would say not. It's like riding a bike. We start with what seems possible and before we know it, we're gaining confidence and pedaling faster than ever. We're riding the wave of life! The truth is that a lot of people never get to that point because they beat themselves down and chicken out while in situations where they might have achieved great success because of their fear of failing. This failure mindset is sometimes educated into us when we are growing up. Still to this day, there are people that the only way to make a solid living is to go to college, finish out with a degree, find a good company to work for, contribute to your 401k, and save every other penny for retirement. They think finding ways to monetize your passion, no matter how unique that may be, isn't secure enough, so you should follow the masses and try living a more "stable" life. Hopefully, no matter what demographic you're in, you can understand why this is a losing mentality and solely living to work a 9-5 for someone else will never help you get ahead in life. I tend to think the reason this crazy mentality even still exists is because so many people are afraid of the unknown, so they would rather build barriers than create a new lifestyle. Dispelling negative self-talk (such as thinking '*I can't do it*') is the first place to start if you're really serious about scaling to new levels in your real estate career. I had a mentor tell me, "*fear and doubt is only created by inactivity.*" If you think about it, those words hold a lot of truth. You'll be surprised how everything becomes easier once you try and achieve something you otherwise thought might be impossible just by taking one small step forward. Any agents who are at the top of lists in their markets right now were just like you when they first started. They were where you are in your career right now, but they chose to believe in themselves and take it day by day and better their craft at every chance they got. That's the exact attitude and approach I cemented in myself when I was getting started. In this line of work, a positive attitude will go a long way because there's always going to be pitfalls that make you want to find the negative and dwell on it. The key is to figure out how to flip the script. Everything is not really a negative, but more of a lesson and how you react to the lesson will determine how soon you'll become successful on your next task and transaction.

I've read that many of the greatest failures are people who didn't know how close they were to success. To illustrate that, think of the example of Thomas Edison and how he had to try 1,000 times before he finally invented the light bulb. If Edison had given up on the 999th time, he would have been a failure (despite his effort and incessant attempts) and nobody would know his name today. Of course, if you failed this much at selling homes, I'd encourage you to think hard about your future in real estate. All I'm saying is that you need to have a go-getter attitude. You have a choice; you can either obsess over where you are now and the challenges you are facing, or you can choose to focus on where you're going and where you want to end up. Only when you choose to focus on where you want to go (and what you want to achieve) will you be able to master the creativity and arsenal of skills you need to get there. Just like a roadmap. So, before you read any further, I want you to take a minute to think about and write down 3 limiting beliefs that might hold back your real estate career. Now, let's write three sentences that flip the script and describe how you WILL overcome those obstacles.

Myth #2 – "It can't be done in my market"
Even agents who believe that something is possible often fall prey to another equally common myth. *"It may be possible, but not in my market"*.
The reasoning here is that to make it happen in your current market, you'd need to have a bigger market share than there ever was before. Just because something has never been done in your market area doesn't mean you can't be the first person to do it. Often, in real estate, no one has the "right" answer. The fact that you haven't found the "right" way to make it work in your market means that you need to start seeking ideas outside of what you already have. Maybe you need to start trying approaches that have worked in other markets? I have known many agents who harbor a lot of potential but they just get stuck with the wrong plan. Once they get out of the one-two-or-three listings per month mindset, they accomplish a lot more.

Myth #3 – "It's Too Much Work"
A lot of agents fear that the more successful they become, the more time and effort they'll need to pour in. They think they would lose their freedom and, therefore, say they are not able to make the sacrifices needed to accomplish the right kind of success. While that can be true if you don't manage your time correctly, the reality is, you can put in 40-hour workweeks and make a meager $40,000 a year working for someone else's dreams or you can invest the same time to make six figures a year working on your own business and dreams.

Whatever approach you are using, we all have the same 24 hours in a day, so the key is to have laser focus on what your goals are and chip away piece by piece. As I said earlier, you need to think of leverage in order to be able to expand your business. Time and effort should be viewed in terms of efficiency. This way, you'll be able to have maximum impact on the time you devote to your business.

Myth #4 – "I'll Lose Money"
Being an overly successful real estate agent has a lot to do with knowing how to operate when the end result is unclear. One of the things I do to dispel this myth is to hold the costs accountable for incremental results. Let's say, for example, I want to invest $5,000 in a website or marketing channel for my business. I'll focus on exploring how that money is going to grow my business, not how it could get lost. And then I'll do the right things to make sure it counts. Successful real estate agents understand the difference between cost and investment. Think about it this way – any dollar spent that increases your profitability is a dollar well-invested.

Myth #5 – "My clients will always work with me"
Even great real estate agents often fall into the entrapment of this myth and, as a result, do not reach their highest potential. However high quality you think your real estate service is, keep in mind that it can always be replicated by others. Basking in the comfort is one way you'll get beat by the competition. Instead, focus on how you can improve your service to your clients. A broker named Vince Leisey once told me a great saying, "Money flows to the different, not the same." What that means is you have to continue to find ways to make yourself stand out in a crowd that looks so similar. Most of the public believes the stigma that all real estate agents are the same. They are lazy and don't work hard. They stick a sign in the yard and the home sells itself. It's up to you to show how and why you're different from the moment they come across your business, whether that be online or in person.

The Success Mindset – 6 Questions to Ask Yourself Right Now

Now, I don't want to bombard you with affirmations and positive thinking clichés, but it definitely takes a certain mindset – and developing the right habits – to unlock your full potential as a real estate agent. Over the years, I have learned that I'm more effective when I think in certain ways that support my goals and efforts. If you just want to be a realtor because it sounds like a cool career, then you are probably going to have a very tough time finding success. But if you're in it for a reason that coincides with your purpose and your "WHY", then you're right on course. I wanted to get into real estate to build relationships with others throughout the industry that allowed me to find more deals to own – not just sell real estate for others. This would allow me to change the foundation and legacy for my family for generations to come. As I have come to realize, ultimate potential is nothing without goals. You might work hard to reach your full potential, but you're going to feel stuck if you don't precisely set goals. That's why this section is important, so you can learn how to think right and how to base your entire business on the right mindset. This way, you'll have a solid foundation to move up the ladder and accomplish new milestones as you gather your bag of tricks later on in this book.

What's your <u>WHY</u> when it comes to real estate?

Early on in my sales career, I read the book by the great Simon Sinek, *Start with Why*. The foundation of the book is the saying, "People don't buy WHAT you do; but WHY you do it." I believe this is an essential question for every real estate agent as well, new or experienced. Knowing your 'Big Why' helps set the right tone for making changes in your daily habits. Most of us fail to move forward on the smallest tasks because of fear, but when we make a mindset shift and reflect on why we're making a particular move, we are able to free up space and move forward. We start to truly understand that fear is a part of the growth process. Without fear we're not uncomfortable so, in essence, we're not stretching ourselves to achieve higher goals. When you know your 'Big Why', you'll find it easier to maintain focus and high energy in the face of any obstacles that will be thrown in your way. Now, get a pen and a piece of paper and write down what motivates or drives you. Don't be afraid to write down many things, but ultimately you want to find your Big Why. Feel free to combine those small motivations into your big motivation. Whether that be family, freedom, balance, whatever it is...Your big why leads to big focus and big energy, whereas those small 'why's' lead to little focus and little energy. When you face your work days with such purpose (propelled by your Big Why), you can go far and wide. So, close your book right now and don't read on until you've figured out your Big Why.

What big goals do you have?

As I said earlier, without setting big goals you can never know where ultimate potential lies. The power behind having big goals is that it requires you to develop big habits (by beginning with the end in mind). Your habits either serve to restrict you to the current level or to propel you to the next one. When you focus on your big goals, you'll be focusing on creating big habits that will help you accomplish your highest levels of success. Small goals always facilitate small habits. Big goals always facilitate big habits.

In his top-rated book, The Power of Habit, Charles Duhigg says that "Champions don't do extraordinary things. They do ordinary things, but they do them without thinking, too fast for the other team to react. They follow the habits they've learned."
What's even more incredible about big goals is that they have a magnetic effect. They tend to pull all the smaller goals along the way without you even noticing. This philosophy is very important in real estate. It's been used by some of the elite agents out there, and everyone else can use it to start their real estate career from a point of strength.

What are the possibilities?

I like to think that real estate is one activity where curiosity does not kill the cat. The more you're curious to learn about selling and buying real estate, the better you'll be able to grasp the ins and outs of the industry. There are no mysteries to success in this field. It's just a matter of thinking of the big picture: setting goals that almost scare you and then being diligent (and smart) for the kind of work it takes to create the success you're looking for.

Francis of Assisi was a 12th-century Italian preacher and deacon. One of his most popular quotes has everything to do with human mindset on possibilities.
"Start by doing what's necessary; then do what's possible and suddenly you are doing the impossible." The reason why this is so powerful is because we all have fears and doubts when we start out. There's so many thoughts that will run through our head about how we can accomplish whatever the goal is. The trick is just to get started. Taking action is never easy, but if we break it up into small actionable plays, we'll suddenly feel like we're moving mountains. Think of it like riding a bike. When you're first learning to ride, you don't think about the miles you can ride across the city. You just try to make it 1 block at a time, then 2 blocks, then, suddenly, before you know it, you've road 2 miles.

Another quote I love is by the late great Henry Ford, *"whether you think you can or you can't, you're right"*. I loved this quote from the moment I first heard it. During my last year at my old brokerage, our broker painted this on the wall of our second floor. I loved walking past it every day because I believed no truer words have ever been spoken. If you believe something is possible, your mind tends to conceive the means necessary to make that possibility a reality. Not surprisingly, the opposite is also true. If you don't believe something is possible, then you will be blind to all the ways it can be done. How interesting things can be!

So, now goes the question, '*Do you think it's possible to become a HIGHLY successful real estate agent/investor?*' When you have possibility, thinking, supporting your big why and big goals, then anything is possible. And that's just it.

Fueled by your big why, big goals, and a World of Possibilities, the next natural thing to do is take action. We all know people who work so hard for something, spend countless hours researching how to get started, and then stall right when they need to take action. We all might be guilty of doing this at one point or the other. No matter how good your big why and big goals are, you need to take action so they can come to fruition. Your big why should give you an action-first mindset and you should be on the lookout for new ways to accomplish your mission. Taking action is a consistent activity. You have to ask yourself what else you can do to move your ship forward, closer to the shore that is your ultimate goal.

Can you sell or will you be sold?

Many people stay away from real estate because they think they can't sell or don't want to be called a "salesman". They are afraid and intimidated because they have poor sales skills. What these people don't realize is that life is all about sales. One of my mentors, Grant Cardone, wrote a great book called "Sell or Be Sold". In the book, he says the number one step in gaining confidence to convert a sale is that you MUST SELL YOURSELF ON WHAT YOU'RE SELLING. It makes total sense when you think about it. If you don't have the confidence and conviction in your service or product, how do you truly expect someone else to? If your body language is off or you're stuttering with your words and have weird energy, especially in this people business, your clients will pick up on it very quickly. You are trying to convince folks to invest in the biggest purchase of their lives. In residential real estate, for sure, this is an emotional purchase. There will be excitement, positivity, nervousness, buyer's remorse, and more, all wrapped up into this transaction. Your clients must feel they've made a solid investment and it starts with your energy to drive the mood. Body language and HOW you say things will be far more important than WHAT you say. You don't have to be the greatest salesman walking on earth in order to be successful in real estate, you just need to be willing to improve on your sales skills daily and it starts with your energy. Understand that people are using you for your knowledge, confidence, and positive energy that you have innately acquired over the years. There's no magic pill. It's all based on confidence. How you gain more confidence? By taking action! The more deals and conversations about real estate you're involved in, the more confidence you'll have to talk about it with others who are depending on your guidance. Always remember, the main things you should focus on when selling anything is your *confidence, brand credibility, energy* and *market knowledge*. Real estate is no different.

As John Mason said, *"the most unprofitable item ever manufactured is an excuse."* So, if you're ready to make it in real estate, stop making excuses and get ready to sell.

The most successful real estate agents know that when it comes to selling real estate, it's all about the relationship (not the transaction). Strive to cultivate a solid relationship with everyone you meet and the business will eventually come to you. There will be agents who you come across and can tell right away are instinctively transactional. They believe that if there's no deal, they don't get paid, so there's no reason to build a relationship based on an abundant mentality. While this approach may be good in the short-term, it won't serve your long-term real estate selling goals. Real estate is a marathon and you have to keep in mind that while someone might not buy from you in the immediate future, that doesn't mean 6-12 months from now you won't be on their mind because you've stayed in contact with them and always delivered value.

When talking to friends, family, and even sellers, agents often hear that they don't have much value because '*the properties sell themselves'*. That's a complete myth. If properties sold themselves, why would any homeowner need to pay 6% or 7% commission to an agent? Just to open the door? I think not. Sellers want to get the best possible price for their home. Savvy real estate agents have the confidence. They fight for their commission and what they're worth because they truly provide that value through pricing the home correctly, marketing through personal and social networks, and serving as a buffer to negotiate the best deals for their clients.

Are you willing to slap your fears?

Fear is perhaps the biggest obstacle people face when they are finally ready to take action. They will stumble into a few obstacles and recoil into fear. They will be paralyzed by the fear of failure and rejection. They will be paralyzed by the fear they could waste all their time and still have nothing to show for it. When fear happens in this way, it stops you right in your tracks. You are done the moment you start to focus on the fear of failure instead of what's possible and the excitement of the end result. In real estate, fear will be the reason you don't get that $10,000 commission. Think about this scenario which happens so often. You have friends who are thinking of selling their home in the next 3-6 months. You are scared to ask for the business because you've talked yourself into "what if they reject my offer of listing their home?" Well, the reality of it is, if this happened, are you any worse off than you were before you asked? Also, if you didn't ask, would you be kicking yourself if they later listed with a complete stranger and you found out the only reason they listed with them is because that agent asked for the business? It's happened to all of us.

One thing I tell people who feel blinded by fear is to stop for a minute and reflect. Ask yourself, *"If I was to fail, what's the worst that could happen? No matter what the worst is...could I bounce back from it?"* 99% of the time you can bounce back without a doubt. Your pride might be hurt, but you'd be stronger in the end. Possibility thinkers believe in what is possible. But you have to go the extra mile and really take action. Taking action means you're going to make some mistakes, and a few times you'll fall short of expectations you had hoped for. Setbacks will happen. But that's how you know that you are doing something...because if you retreated into your comfort zone, you wouldn't have the opportunity of making mistakes. Momentary setbacks should be seen for what they are – learning opportunities. So, never let the fear of failure stop you.

If you're ready to be a super successful real estate agent in your town, metro, or even the whole state – start seeing fear for what is: False Evidence Appearing Real.

Are you making progress?

Most often, success breakthroughs come from effort and persistence. Thomas Edison had to try 999 times before he could get his breakthrough. Think about all that effort and all the knowledge he accumulated. You can think the same way when it comes to real estate. If you spend all your time planning this and planning that but doing nothing, then you aren't going to make any breakthroughs. It's the action that you take that matters. So, get ready to go out there, knock on doors, and start more conversations – because that's how you get business.

Every minute you spend out there trying to get new business is a minute that counts. That's how you're going to learn new things and accomplish new milestones. I would also like to point out that the most successful real estate agents are people who think strategically and competitively. Think about the last time you played a game of chess (or whatever other mind game) with a friend. You were determined to beat them, right? Maybe because of your pride – you wanted to have the upper hand. Or maybe because you simply hate losing. Whatever the reason may be, you should have the same attitude when it comes to real estate. Think 2 steps ahead. Think strategically. I'll evoke the Pareto principle here again. Are you among the 'real estate crowd' that's doing the same basic stuff and hoping to get results. Or are you the few who are playing the winning game by doing what really matters. Successful agents are strategic and competitive, and strategic thinking has a lot to do with making sure you're doing the 20% that matters so you get 80% of the results you want. It's about outdoing your competitors in a big way and thinking ahead. Again, here comes the difference between rules and winning. Our rules in the industry have nothing to do with winning. They are about conduct and ethics. Similar to taking real estate classes: any agent who has passed their real estate exam will tell you that test has nothing to do with building relationships and selling real estate. It's to keep your from breaking the law and ending up in front of the real estate commission board. Just because you have mastered the protocols, ethics and conduct doesn't mean you're winning…because winning is a different game altogether. So, don't break the rules, but make sure you focus on how you are going to win.

Chapter 3:

Lead Generation is the Key

When I started out as a real estate agent, I had a tough time figuring out where to start with prospecting. I had zero clients, zero spheres of influence, and very big goals. I was determined to grow from being a real estate beginner to a real estate champion. I had promised myself that I would make six figures during my first year but, of course, that was easier said than done. I knew that prospecting (finding clients) was instrumental to success in any business. Real estate was no different.

Like many new agents, my first prospecting efforts involved calling FSBOs, expired listings, and anyone I could get on the phone. During my first week I decided to commit an hour to this every morning. I was getting a lot of contacts but because I was new in the business and hadn't mastered the scripts for real estate objections, I wasn't getting much traction on finding a 'now' client. I decided to switch it up and put my energy into doing open houses. My thoughts were, if when I was face to face, people would be able to see my energy and excitement for what I was talking about and then I could follow up after I had already built rapport. It wasn't easy to get my first few clients, but eventually, I did. My first two deals and clients came from a new construction open house. Here's how it happened, I was on my third week of open houses with no strong lead for 'now' clients yet. About an hour into my 2-hour open house, a nice young-looking couple came into my $425,000 new construction model. Being that it was $425,000 and the average home price in my market was $190,000, I wasn't jumping joy thinking they would be doing anything more than "just looking". Still, I chose not to judge and I focused on building rapport. While asking qualifying and relationship building questions, I asked if they were already pre-approved or had a lender in mind that they would use when they found their dream home. Mr. Buyer stated he did have someone in mind who did refinance when he owned a home a couple years back. I told them I had a great lender who I'd recommend and, if nothing else, they could compare to make sure they were getting the best rate and deal possible. They were totally fine with that. After getting them to leave their contact information on the sign-in sheet, I followed up immediately after the open house and connected them with my lender. Coincidently and crazy enough, IT WAS THE SAME LENDER that did Mr. Buyer's refinance! This helped me build immediate credibility and 3 weeks later, I was able to help them land their dream home under contract for $405,000. That meant my first commission check was over $10,000! BOOM! The point of telling that story is to explain that while you must always be lead generating there's no right way, and not everything is for everyone. I knew I needed to get face to face to build relationships faster with my potential clients. If you focus on being authentic to who you are and doing the necessary daily activities, everything else will fall into place. I learned early on that when you establish the right routine and stick to it, things seem to happen for you. For me, that open house routine got me kick-started and because I was taking action, it built my confidence. I also became more efficient with my time. I started out doing opens for 2-3 hours but noticed I was getting the same results doing them only for an hour and a half. My first would be noon to 1:30PM and the second would be 2:00-3:30PM. I chose two homes with different price points, one new construction with a higher price point and one existing home under $250k. By finishing up around 3:30 or even 4PM, it allowed me to still have time to head back to the office after and enter all my new prospects into my CRM and follow up, all the while being home by 5PM to spend the rest of Sunday evening with my family.

I learned that prospecting had more to do with my vision of success than I thought. It required a positive mindset. I've seen agents who would set up their website, join service organizations, wear name badges, put stickers on their rides, share their business cards, and respond to emails. But I somehow knew that this wasn't enough. It was just what everyone else was doing. This was the

80% that only generated 20% of the results. I understood that to really get high-quality leads, I had to make it more specific and personable than that. I had to do what really matters. Things like coffee and lunches, first time home buyer seminars, Facebook live Q&A, these were the ways I could be different and really gain an edge on my competition.

There's 2 sides of the coin with prospecting

The goal of prospecting is to develop a database of likely clients and then systematically communicate with them in the hopes of converting them from potential clients to current and clients.

As a real estate agent, there are two types of clients that you can pursue: listings and buyers.

You can generate listing leads by referrals, knocking on doors, networking events, organizing open houses, calling your sphere of influence, targeting FSBO conversions, and being a part of tips groups: just to name a few ways. As I mentioned earlier, listing clients (sellers) are more valuable than buyers, so they should form the core of your prospecting strategy. The thing with this kind of client though is that they rarely come without an effort from you. Why? The public perception of a real estate agent is someone who puts people in their car and drives them around, showing them homes they could buy. That's why you'll notice that when people send you referrals, they are often sending you prospective buyers.

Lead generation for listings is an ongoing effort. You have to use your networking skills and ask those within your circle of influence to share names of people they might know who are looking to sell a piece of real estate. I have also realized that developing a specialty as a listing agent really helps. This means having to work with any expired FSBO listings you can get your hands on, and basically letting people know that you're the person to call whenever they need to sell a home. This must be communicated to everyone you meet and efforts must be prioritized based on the probability of success.

1. Prospecting for buyers tends to be much easier starting out compared to prospecting for sellers.

It's often easier to get buyer referrals. Open houses work pretty well to attract buyers. Open houses are a time-tested strategy that every real estate agent should be using. It's what I used to pick up my first clients. If you find that you're low on buyers, consider increasing the frequency of your open houses. Keep in mind that the kind of houses and price points you choose will have a major impact on the type of buyers you attract. If you focus on higher end property or new construction homes, you'll find that you tend to attract buyers on that level.

Planning more open houses in the low range to attract first-time buyers may help your business grow faster. First-time buyers are good because they tend to buy more quickly. They've also never owned a home before or worked with another real estate agent, so you have a better chance to cultivate a great long-term agent relationship. If you offer a good service to the first-time buyer, you can win their loyalty and establish a valuable life-long relationship. Also, buyers eventually turn into sellers which means if you've stayed in touch, they'll be calling you when they decided they want to upgrade in 5-7 years.

Major key: Home buyers, especially first-time buyers, will be on cloud 9 after you've helped them seal the deal on their dream home and would love to help repay you however they can. Where I've learned most agents have the highest success is in asking their clients to refer them to friends, relatives, and anyone else they know who might be interested in a home as well, right before their deal has closed: that's the time when their energy is so positive and life hasn't gotten hectic with moving and decorating yet.

2. Prospecting for hot seller leads

Most agents are on the lookout for the "*hot shop*" property. These are usually homes and other pieces of real estate that are likely to sell fast because of their location, style, and resale values in their area. The ability to differentiate between good, great, and even bad listings can be tough in the beginning but usually will become easier with years of experience. More times than not, every listing is at least a good listing. What makes a listing great or bad is the expectations of the seller. All properties can offer a lot of value to buyers depending on price and condition. If the seller has a fixer-upper home and wants top dollar because that's what their neighbor got, it's on you as the agent to set the right expectation and have that tough conversation with your clients.

Government assistance programs are also a great place to look for hot properties. Such programs are usually meant to help low-income families and seniors. As the country's population ages, seniors are demanding more services – including housing. There are easier financing terms for this group and you can pounce in and turn seniors into a substantive target audience.

Watch your local newspaper for bargains. It's common that when sellers are nearly giving up, they'll place their ads in the community paper as a last-ditch effort, especially for older sellers. When people are desperate to sell, they tend to be very flexible. This makes it easier for you to negotiate an excellent deal.

Even in a seller's market there are ways to be more creative and stand out to gain more listings. Some of those are:

- Grabbing nosey neighbor sellers at open houses
- Door knocking in a hot neighborhood after a home was sold for more than the asking price.
- Zillow 'Make Me Move' listings (those sellers have indicated they want to move)
- Finding homes "for rent" in a hot neighborhood with great sales activity.
- Facebook ads with landing pages that forward to home evaluations.

The Three-Fold Prospecting Plan

Since prospecting is an ongoing effort in the real estate business, you want to find long-term success. Apply the following 3-step plan to make the most out of your real estate prospecting.

ONE: Prospect daily

The most successful agents I've ever come across prospect daily. You don't work your prospecting around your day – you work your day around your prospecting. For most agents, when they first decide to pursue their license, it's because they have big goals and dreams and truly believe real estate with all its financial benefits can help them achieve it. The thing is they lack the knowledge of understanding how much effort and energy goes into finding new clients and closing deals. The major secret to how you will get the new house, car, and investment properties you want? Prospecting. How effective you are at generating leads and finding clients will determine how successful you are as a real estate agent. Again, this is where forming a habit becomes crucial. You must find ways to keep your pipeline full. If you're relying on one or two clients to come through, it can be a long and emotional roller coaster. The more contacts you make through prospecting, the sooner you'll start to consistently close more deals.

I've found that it works best if you find a set time to prospect daily controlled environments where all your prospecting tools are available. If you have a home-based office, make it valuable by bringing a computer, telephone, headset, and a stand-up area. You might want to tack a few scripts on the wall for contacting FSBO prospects or past clients. Basically, the goal is to make your office a comprehensive resource for your prospecting efforts.

TWO: Kill distractions

Distractions are the enemy of productivity.
Have you ever played the popular smartphone game called 'Angry Birds'? Believe it or not, this little addictive game leads to over $1.5 billion in productivity loss for businesses across the country.

How so? Because folks are always playing Angry Birds at the office while they should be working.

All of us have our own distractions. Maybe it's the video games. Maybe you're always checking your social media timelines. It might be that you have an app on your phone that eats so much of your attention. The truth of the matter is that a lot of agents welcome distractions that take them away from the task of the moment – prospecting.

Establishing productive routines and habits is very important to your success as a real estate agent. Start by making cutting those distractions out of your life when you need to be focusing on your business. Some of the things you can do are to put your phone on silent mode, turn off the email notification, and tell people who want to meet during your prospecting hours that you already have an appointment. Think about what measures you can take to reduce distractions so you can prospect productively.

THREE: Follow the plan

Are you taking the right steps in the right order? That's what it takes to succeed. Establishing and maintaining a predetermined routine is very important when it comes to prospecting. You must know who you are going to call for the day, and why. Consider creating a list of things you are going to do the night before: when you wake up in the morning, you'll only need to review your calls, daily goals and you'll be ready to go. Do proper research to make sure that you have the right scripts, dialogues, and objection handling strategies. There's also dialers like Mojo and RedX, as well as lists you can plug into them so it doesn't eat up all of your time trying to hunt and type in phone numbers.

Stay faithful to your daily objectives so that you always finish what you start. If your goal is to make 10 contacts for the day, deliver on that. Don't get to four and then let your mental process get in the way. Learning to do things with a strict discipline will make things happen in this line of work.

Increase your efficiency

How efficient do you believe you can be in real estate prospecting? Your efficiency level will have a major influence on the volume of sales you can generate for your business.
I was once browsing on Quora.com when I came across an interesting answer to the question *'why do some people succeed in life and others don't?'* One of the answers, Johann Joubert, introduced a concept known as **"The Potato Effect"**.

Two guys – Pete and John – started working at a company on the same day.
Five years later, Pete requested a sit down with his boss. During the meeting, he asked his boss why he was on the same level as when he started whilst John was already in management.

The boss said that he would explain but only if Pete would run down to the vegetable shop on the corner to find out if they had potatoes for sale.
Pete ran as quickly as he could and when he got back to the office he proudly exclaimed that they did in fact have potatoes for sale.

The boss asked how much they were so Pete hurried back to the shop and when he came back he told his boss that they had large potatoes for only $10 per bag.
The boss then asked if they didn't have smaller bags. Pete, once again, rushed back to the shop and on his return told his boss that they did in fact have smaller bags at only $7 per bag.

The boss then asked if they were washed or unwashed and after Pete went back to the shop he explained that they had both washed and unwashed available.
The boss then asked him to call John to the office.
When John arrived, the boss asked him to go to the vegetable shop and find out if they had potatoes for sale.
When John arrived back his answer was:

They do have potatoes for sale, both in large and small bags at only $10 for the large ones and $7 for the smaller ones. One can also choose between washed and unwashed potatoes.
The boss then asked Pete if he now understood why John reached the higher levels while he didn't.

You might be Pete who has to go out four times to gather the information needed. But as you work your way up, you want to be John who does things more effectively. Of course, you are going to have to meet some challenges. Maybe the potato shop owner has to finish serving two customers in line before he can answer all your questions. But once you learn to overcome your challenges, there will be no limits to how far you can go.

One of the most common challenges real estate agents face with lead generation is sustaining a solid program that consistently increases leads. Most agents tend to wander off once they have generated a relatively high number of leads. They settle down and devote their time and energy to servicing the available business. By taking their eyes off the ball, they neglect their lead generation program.
This is a common booby trap that I tell agents to watch out for. No matter how much business you have right now, there's nothing that could overshadow the potential of lead generation. In fact, I like to say that prospecting sits at the very top of the real estate business food chain. It's the one thing you should always work for and that should never stop. Thinking about it, it might appear like there's no harm done stopping your lead generation program for a while. But that's not the reality. When you stop your lead generation, it loses its momentum. When it loses its momentum, it's not going to be as effective.

Successful agents will never abandon their lead generation. They understand that a systematic, consistent, and sustained prospecting program is crucial to their long-term success. Dealing with today's business should never take precedence over growing tomorrow's business.

Tracking and converting leads is another common prospecting challenge agents face. Generating leads is not enough on its own. You've got to follow up and turn them into appointments. These appointments should then allow you to close the leads into business. Keen attention to tracking. And lead generation is a core discipline for lead generation. If you do the work to acquire leads and then fail to follow up, that's money you are leaving on the table.

As your business grows, you might find that you are overwhelmed by all the tasks. This could be a signal you need to bring in a helping hand. If you hire an employee, my advice would be to hire a part-time assistant first or a transaction coordinator; this will free you up to focus less of your time on paperwork and the non-business generating activities. There are multiple suggestions on how to pay, but the more popular one is a small base salary with bonus incentives or a pay-per-transaction structure. Always use an effective tracking system to make sure they really are adding value to your business.

Hiring an assistant is the first step to building a team. An assistant will create or manage your budget, manage incoming calls, schedule appointments, implement and monitor market programs, prepare legal documents, coordinate your schedule, set up open houses, create warm call lists, and much more. Don't see the assistant as an expense; they are an investment in yourself, your clients, and your brand. If you're already crying out for help, this is one of the best investments you could make. Your assistant can also help track the numbers so you focus on the activities that count to drive business. Many agents are still trapped in spur-of-the-moment kind of marketing and prospecting. They will go for the latest and greatest lead generation program. They are tempted by marketing programs that dangle the bait of instant success. This is not unusual because any form of marketing works – just not everywhere and for everyone. But it is also not how you win in the game to be a super successful real estate agent. The best approach is to meticulously prospect and market over time, then track your results.

Tracking is what you need to weigh the true costs of your plan. You will be able to calculate the cost of acquiring one lead and figuring out the merits of any particular method. Successful real estate agents are willing to be continuous students of their lead generation program.

→ **Work smarter**

Would you rather make non-stop random calls over an 8-hour period, or make a few targeted calls over 15 minutes? Few people would even consider the nonstop calls method. I know you wouldn't either. Because lead generation is not about how many potentials you are able to call, it's about how many people you are able to bring onboard. If I spend 20 minutes on lead generation per day and secure 2 clients, then I'm doing better than the agent who spends 2 hours and scores 2 clients. It means 1 hour of their time is worth one lead, but only 10 minutes of my time is needed to generate one lead. Working smarter trumps working harder – any day!

Your lead generation plan is only as effective as its ability to generate qualified prospects (people who are interested in what you have to offer, need the services you provide, and are able to become a client of yours).

One thing I tell my coaching clients and members on my team is to start small, then build up. This is very important when it comes to lead generation. I'll tell them to start with – let's say – 5 contacts in a day. Note that there's a difference between a contact and a lead. A contact is someone who expresses interest when you dialogue with them on the phone. If you make a call and the babysitter picks up the phone, that is not a contact. With 5 contacts per day, you'd have 25 at the end of the week. It might take you a few weeks before you get the hang of it and are able to gather at least 5 contacts on a daily basis. This kind of momentum is self-motivating. It'll help you get into the habit and make it a daily routine. Only then can we think about increasing the daily target to, let's say, 7 contacts.

Once you can comfortably net 5 contacts per day, the goal is to establish at least one lead daily. Leads are the contacts who have clearly demonstrated that they have a basic motivation and desire to make a change in their living arrangement. This is someone who is interested in either buying or selling a home. The next step is to schedule an appointment with them. During the face-to-face meeting, you get to discuss their needs and wants and learn their why's for wanting to buy or sell real estate. You'll also be able to gauge their commitment and interest in working with you. The appointment gives you an opportunity to kick-start the agent-client relationship. You might want to secure at least one appointment per week.

Now, you might be thinking... *"all those calls for just one appointment?"* Remember that these are just starting goals. It works best when you start small then scale up, not the other way around. Too many agents burn out quickly when trying to generate leads because their expectations are very unrealistic. It's no wonder real estate has one of the highest attrition rates. Trust me, you'll start to see the successful agents that record award after award in your town, they got there by starting off small and keeping consistent while building skills in their lead generation. This strategy will give any agent the solid foundation they need to expand their business to 6 figures in the first 12 months. Think about it: let's say you set up 100 appointments throughout the year. If you were able to convert 50% of those into clients and closed business (50 deals) and your commission was only $3,000 on average, you'd still have made $150,000 gross commission at the end of the year. Combine this with making sound money decisions and getting your business under the right tax entity (find a great CPA), what could these numbers do for your family?

Chapter 4:

Discipline Wins Championships

When I was younger, I remember my grandma would always tell me, "A hard head makes a soft a**!" I never knew what she really meant by that until I got older and had my a** handed to me a couple of times. She would try to give me the knowledge about whatever it was that I was trying to do but, of course, I never took heed to the advice because I thought I knew it all already. I always had to find out the hard way even though I knew that since she had so much more wisdom, she had to know what she was talking about. Even when I knew she was 100% right, being as foolish as I was, I still wasn't disciplined enough to take the advice and switch up my path. This is the same mindset that can hold you back in real estate.

Have you ever wondered why some do 10+ million in volume every single year with no team and sometimes no assistant, while others struggle to even make real estate a full-time income? The answer is one word: **discipline**. As crazy as it may sound, most agents are not disciplined enough to prospect, follow up, time-block, and nurture relationships. Imagine someone told you that if you just did these 4 things you could have anything you wanted in this world? Money, time, recognition, you could have it all. That's exactly what's at stake in real estate.

To get and stay ahead of the curve in real estate you must have an open and innovative mindset, and you must always be prospecting. Prospecting at least 2 hours a day will help you accelerate your book of business and referrals 3-4 times faster than the average agent in your market. That's one of the beauty marks of real estate as well, it doesn't matter what market you're in if you're willing to put the work into building relationships (both with clients and agents). Be disciplined in your daily habits and there's no way you won't succeed.

I was fortunate enough to grasp the concept early on in my career, that the prospecting I did each day was for 30-60 even 90 days on out. By prospecting deliberately for just 2 hours a day, I could ensure that I was always going to have something in my pipeline. Most agents don't prospect every single day. That's the reason their real estate career is characterized by up-and-down fluctuations in income. Prospecting daily doesn't have to be in the form of just phone calls only. You can prospect at local networking events, on social media, coffee and lunches, hair appointments, mastermind groups, and more. The main goal is to just continue adding leads and prospects to your pipeline. Let's be honest, not being consistent is the reason most agents aren't successful. It's not because they don't want to do more business, it's because they're not disciplined enough to continuously find more clients to keep adding to their pipeline.

Michael Jordan once said that he missed over 9,000 shots in his career. He never focused on the misses, he simply embraced the journey but, more importantly, stayed committed to the destination. That's what real estate is all about. Making the phone calls, doing the coffee and lunches, open houses, client pop-ups. No one likes to do these tasks week in, week out, but the top agents know that this is how to flip the game and have future business chasing after you – rather than you chasing after it.

Coach, Tim Harris, says, *"It's all about doing what you don't want to do, when you don't want to do it, at the highest level."* If you think about it, that's the mentality of any great achiever in any industry.

You may note that a good deal of what I emphasize in this book has to do with self-mastery and mindset. That's because success in real estate is predominantly about self-mastery. Everyone is aware of the concept of discipline, but very few people truly understand it. Discipline is indeed what separates the good from the great. It's vital to everyone from toddlers to seniors, and without it, we would all be chaos. Think about it, who can you think of that you have looked up to and is wildly successful that hasn't displayed discipline?

One thing I have come to appreciate about discipline is that it gives you mastery over yourself, your schedule, and all areas of your life. And this is not only specific to real estate. It's gospel whether you are a school teacher, a pilot, or a handyman. Discipline will push you to work hard because you know that's what you need to prosper. It'll push you to go out and start networking with people and selling homes instead of sitting on the couch or gossiping all day long.

Lack of willpower can be a major challenge for beginner real estate agents. When you are new and struggling to make your first few transactions, it's easy to fall back and relax. Discipline will help you start doing things in a new way – the best way.

Simple Hacks for Getting Disciplined

Now that we've talked about how important discipline is to your success in real estate, it's time to see how you can get into the play. Scientific research shows that willpower is strongest in the morning. It declines throughout the course of the day. That's why so many agents like to make their prospecting calls first thing in the morning. There's less distractions and you're fresh off a night of rest so you feel re-energized. Discipline helps you stick to what you need to do even when your willpower is drying up.

We live in a highly interconnected world with so much social media shoved in our faces every day and this can either be an advantage or a disadvantage. You can use the Internet to increase visibility for your business, but you can also use it as a time killer. I wanted to share with you some tips to stay disciplined so you can attain success as a real estate agent.

a.) Surround yourself with a supportive environment

Even the most disciplined of us experience a willpower break once in a while. So, it's crucial that you create an environment that supports you, continually pushes you in a forward direction, and knows your goals. The environment you are in will have a major impact on whether or not you can achieve your goals consistently at the highest level.

Let's say, for example, that you're trying to lose weight and get fitter. The kind of environment you surround yourself with will have a major impact on your prospects of success. Think about it. If you surround yourself with people who are eating all types of junk and don't care about your plans, it's probably going to be a lot harder for you to achieve your goal. But if you surround yourself with the right crowd (people who are disciplined and invest their effort into helping you achieve your goals) and you also get rid of junk food in your kitchen – you'll be moving in the right direction.

The same is true when you want to achieve goals in real estate and are trying to discipline yourself. You've got to get rid of the social distractions, physical barriers, distance, or psychological constraints that make it hard for you to stick to your daily tasks at hand. Ways to do this is to find an accountability partner and arrange to get together at least 2 times a week and prospect for new clients or even give past clients a call. You can do this for 30 minutes to an hour and add an incentive on it. Say if you're doing it on Mondays, Wednesdays, and Fridays at 11AM, whoever gets the least amount of leads buys the other lunch that day. The goal is to make sure you have someone in your corner who knows your goals and believes in your potential. This way, even if you're having an off day as we all do, this person won't allow you to wallow in your fears or pity party but help to motivate you and get you back on track fast.

b.) Prioritize critical tasks

In his bestselling book, *"Eat That Frog"*, author, Brian Tracy, states the importance of prioritizing tasks. If the first thing you do in the morning is eat a live frog, then you can go through the rest of the day with the satisfaction of knowing that it is probably the worst thing that can happen all day. In this case, 'eating the frog' is your biggest, most important task. That one task that you are most likely to procrastinate on – unless you do something about it!
Complete critical tasks when you have the greatest willpower and motivation. I know that willpower is highest early on in the day – so I'll try to squeeze all my critical tasks into that part of the day. I'll focus on all prospecting (lead generation) tasks during this time. I'll also get started with any job that requires a lot of effort. This clears the rest of my day for easier things. Focus on the 3 most important tasks that have to be done each day. Once you get them out of the way, the rest tends to fall in place.

c.) Plan each day

Planning your day the night before often works out great. The goal is to make a detailed task list (including the time frames) the night before. This will help make your day's schedule ahead as opposed to running up and down in no particular order. When you're first starting out in real estate this is going to be very important: here's why. Nowadays with technology being so instant and clients being able to find homes on their own on Zillow or Realtor.com, they can instantly shoot over a question to you of when they can get in there. If you've planned your day the night before, you'll know what time slots you have available. I have also found out that when you spend a little time to pre-plan your day, you tend to be more productive. Your task list should show expected tasks in terms of priority so you know what to focus on first. You can use a smartphone app with useful to-do list functionality to get things done like Todoist, Wunderlist, and many others that are out there. The most important thing is finding something that works best for you.

One of the best quotes that has stuck with me to this day is, *"If you don't have a plan, you're planning to fail"*. Spending a small fraction of your time (the night before) to pre-plan your day will go a long way to help you make more out of each day.

d) Start small, start with what you have now.

Getting started is often the most difficult part of any task. We put up these barriers in our minds like, "what if this doesn't work?" most of which, the things we tell ourselves are only blocks to keep us in our comfort zone. But once you get started, it's easier to keep going. That's where being disciplined and keeping your promises comes in. The best agents are able to spend 2-5 hours on lead generation every day.

There Is More Than One Way To Prospect

Now, this can seem like a momentous task for beginners and people who are not used to this kind of an activity, but you have to remember: there's more than one way to prospect. There are phones calls, network meetings after hours, door knocking, social media, open houses, coffees, lunches, and many others. The best part about the methods I named above is that most, if not all, cost little to no money. Think about it, you can spend one hour a day prospecting 3-5 people asking them to meet for coffee and let them know how excited you are about this new real estate career and how you can serve them if they need anything. Even if you are starting out with no money, if you arrive five minutes early, you can grab a water and let them know you're good on coffee. Let's even say you met with 3 people a day for 5 days a week. With coffee being $5 a cup, after one month, you've spent less than $250 and if you were to land one deal, you would probably make around a 10x return on your investment after closing the sale.

Open houses are another lucrative and inexpensive way to build your client database quickly. Whether you're on a team or by yourself, shoot an email out to your brokerage or even across your

MLS. Let agents know that you're available to hold any open houses if they need your help. While a lot of the time the norm is to only host open houses for agents within your brokerage, most agents would gladly welcome someone else freeing up their time to do an open house. More importantly, it pleases the seller that the open house will be going on as well. Depending on the agent, you may be able to get them to throw an ad in the newspaper or sponsor a Facebook ad post for the open house. By that Friday, make sure to have your signs up in the neighborhood touting the open house. You could even walk the street on Friday night for one hour being a nosey neighbor to gain more awareness. On Saturday, put a post on your Facebook business page about the open house and share it to your personal page and local area's Facebook groups as well. By the time it's Sunday, everything is ready and you can even take the time to have a nice breakfast with your family before heading out.

So, as you can see, there are many ways to get started with building your database without a lot of money. The most important thing is to just start with smaller promises to yourself that are easier to keep, not big ones that can be overwhelming or currently out of your budget. From day one, tell yourself you're going to prospect at least 15 minutes a day. After about 3 weeks of fulfilling your promise, you'll have the discipline you need to increase the deliverable. You can upgrade to 30 minutes of lead generation daily, and then eventually work all the way up to 4 hours within just a few months.

1. Don't worry if it doesn't feel right

Charles Duhigg, author of **The Power of Habit**, explains that behaviors are handled by a part of the brain known as the basal ganglia. This section is usually also associated with memories, patterns, and emotions. Decisions are handled by a part of the brain known as the prefrontal cortex, which is a totally different area. When a behavior becomes a habit, we stop using the decision-making part of the brain and instead function on auto-pilot.

To form a good habit, you'll need to use the decisions part of the brain until it becomes an habit. This is precisely why it might feel wrong while you try to get into new routines. The brain wants to stay in the comfort zone and do what it's already been programmed to do. So, don't worry if it doesn't feel right as you try to form new, constructive habits. Keep going and you'll be doing them before you even know it.

2. Make sure you reward yourself

Dog trainers use a reward-system to model behavior. They will reward a correct move to reinforce correct/positive behavior. The same psychology can be applied as you work on your self-discipline. We feel motivated when we are rewarded. Schedule a breakfast treat or reward yourself in any other way when you make progress. Maybe you've stuck to your goal of generating leads for at least 30 minutes for an entire month. Before you make a new promise, reward yourself for delivering on your last one. Self-discipline can be hard, so rewarding your effort makes it easier.

The end goal of discipline is that it helps you build healthy habits, routines and rituals around your real estate business. You're going to fail if running your business feels like a struggle. And that's where discipline comes in. Habits, routines and rituals require no willpower. You are essentially putting much of your business life on autopilot. You can save your willpower for other challenges that pop up along the way.

Chapter 5:

Real Estate is a Contact Sport

Agents practicing real estate at the highest level understand real estate is a contact sport. It might revolve around land and buildings, but it's all about dealing with people. Proper communication and negotiation is the energy that oils the real estate business.

Whether you're a solo agent or have a team behind you, your success will come down to how and how many people you interact with. If people like, trust and believe in you, they'll be lining up to do deals with you. And let me be clear. This isn't about being a phony, manipulative salesperson. It's about honesty and integrity. It's about knowledge, confidence, and an ability to build relationships based on trust and being able to serve people at a very professional level. Think about relationships. Most of the time when there's a conflict in a relationship, it's because of a failure to communicate.

John Gottman, a renowned relationship expert, studied couples for decades while trying to figure out why so many marriages ended in divorce. With a 93 percent accuracy, Gottman found that **criticism, defensiveness, contempt and stonewalling** were the four major factors that led to divorce. He called them the '*Four Horsemen of the Apocalypse*'. You might have noticed that all these revolve around communication. Stonewalling, defensiveness, and criticism are defects of communication. This just shows how important communication is in maintaining relationships.

Think about it in the real estate sense. Let's say you are selling a home and you don't set the expectations right or communicate all issues to the buyer. Eventually, they are going to face the issues you didn't point out to them as they settle in their new home.

Naturally, they'll criticize your work, and you'll probably slide into the defensive mode. Worse still, if there are any legal ramifications stemming from this standoff then the real estate commission could have you in contempt and you could be stonewalled from practicing real estate anymore. That one straight shot at communication (or the lack thereof) can single-handedly make or break your real estate dreams.

Active listening

The first element of good communication that you should master as an agent is active listening. You've got to listen in a way that says you understand what the client is saying and show it.

Active listening isn't rocket science. It's something everyone can learn and actually turn into a habit with a little bit of practice. It's listening to hear rather than to speak. We all know someone who constantly finishes someone else's sentences. The reason is because they aren't patient enough to listen to hear and not have a rebuttal. Active listening will help you build better relationships, solve problems in your interactions with clients, and ensure understanding. It will help you do a better job because you have comprehended everything your seller listings and buyer prospects asked of you. Below are a few tips that you can use to be a better active listener:

A. Always face the speaker and maintain eye contact

Have you ever found yourself in a situation where you were talking to someone and all they were doing is gazing out, studying a computer screen, or scanning the room? How did it feel? It's like trying to hit at a moving target. You might have felt that it was a total waste of time. That's exactly what clients would feel like if you didn't pay attention to them when they were talking. However good you are at finding leads and marketing your real estate agency, it's how you communicate with people that's going to determine whether you walk out with an empty promise or a signed contract.

If you're talking to your kid and they just give you half of their attention, you might demand that they look at you. That's how you might react. When a client notices that an agent is not paying full attention, they'll react by looking for another agent.

But just how do you show your client that you're listening and paying attention to them? Agents who are good communicators always face their clients and make eye contact. In Western culture, eye contact is a major ingredient of effective communication. We look each other in the eye when we talk. This is non-negotiable when it comes to communicating with your prospects. Always turn to face them and make eye contact while you converse. Avoid holding your phone, handout or book in between you and the person speaking. Body language: experts say, that when you hold anything (even a cup of coffee) in front of you, you're subconsciously trying to put a barrier between you and the other person. You do not want to make the impression that you're shy, uncertain, or embarrassed. Making eye contact and standing (or sitting) in such a way that you're facing the other person shows that you are interested in what they have to say.

B. Be relaxed and attentive

Now that you're making eye contact with your prospect, simply relax and focus. You don't have to stare fixedly at the other person, you can look away every now and then, naturally. The important thing is paying attention and focusing on being present. This means you have to get rid of distractions that might be competing for your attention. If your phone or smart watch is beeping with social media notifications every minute or so, put it on silent mode. Or have you noticed that the speaker (your prospect) has a funny accent? That's a mental distraction. Any thoughts, feelings, or biases that might be getting in the way of you paying attention should be screened out so that time you're zoned in.

C. Keep your mind open

You are communicating with your listing or buyer client so that you can fulfill a specific objective. If it's the buyer, you want them to commission you as the agent who'll finally help them find a house to buy. If it's the seller, you want a signed agreement to help them sell the home. To accomplish your objective, you need to keep an open mind during the communication. It's not uncommon that the prospect will say things you would mentally criticize. If they say or do something you'd consider stupid, it's okay to be alarmed, but don't say to yourself, *"Well, that was a stupid move."* As long as you start engaging in this kind of judgmental bemusement, you'll have compromised your effectiveness as an active listener.

Agents who are good listeners never jump to conclusions. They know that they are communicating to help their client meet their needs. The only way you'll be able to understand what the client thinks and feels is by paying full attention to what they are saying. You need to slow down your thinking so you can accommodate what they are saying.

D. Avoid interrupting or imposing your 'solutions'

You probably already know how important it is to talk less and listen more when communicating with your clients. It helps to hit the "mute" button. Ever watched one of those TV interviews where everybody was loud and aggressive, like they were all talking at the same time? You don't want your interaction with real estate prospects to be like that. If you interrupt them while they are in the process of saying something, you're basically sending a message that you are more important than them, or that you don't have time for their opinion. However good a solution you already have for your client's needs, it'll never good enough if you have to shut them down in order to share it.

E. Ask clarifying questions during the pause

Wait for the prospect to pause so you can seek clarification. If there's something you didn't quite understand, you might say something along the lines of... *"back up a second, I didn't understand what you just said about..."*
The kind of questions you ask should only be those that help you gain a better understanding. Have you ever been highlighting your favorite movie to a friend only for them to cut you off asking whether you've watched a totally unrelated movie that they consider their favorite? These kinds of sideshow questions are not welcome in an active listening scenario. So, only ask clarifying questions that are on topic.

F. Take notes

Taking notes is another major active listening hack that I use all the time. Your client is communicating a lot of information when talking to you. Even if you normally take notes in your head, just the sight of you jotting down information as they are talking can really help your clients feel like you're already taking your job seriously. There are many ways to take notes nowadays, whether you use your iPad, cell phone, Evernote app, Google Docs or anything else you might like. The main goal is to make sure you're at least recording it somewhere. I'll always put all the critical points of the conversation in bullets that I can review later.

G. Show empathy

A little empathy can go a long way towards reinforcing communication. Did your client just say something that makes them joyous? Make sure you replicate a little bit of that joy. The goal is not to behave like a Hollywood actor. You want to try and show them that you can relate with what they are saying. Use your words and facial expressions to show empathy.

Try to put yourself in the other person's shoes and feel what they might be feeling at that moment. This is the biggest transaction they'll most likely make in their lifetime. It'll take a little bit of concentration and energy on your part to do this (especially if empathy is a rare quality for you), but to your clients, you'll appear more generous and helpful.

"Empathy is indeed the heart and soul of good listening."

H. Pay attention to nonverbal cues

Did you know that up to 93% of all human communication is nonverbal? What am I saying? The words we use contribute to only 7% of the message we convey. How you stand (posture), how you walk, how you use your face and hands while communicating says a lot more than your words do. A good agent will be able to tell they've got a deal just by studying the body language of the prospect.

Have you ever wondered why most salespeople tend to be so convincing? One of the reasons is because they use body language to their advantage. They convey confidence and assurance in what they are saying. They even mirror your own non-verbal cues so that you feel like you have a connection. Perhaps you should spend a few minutes of your time every day to master body language. There are *very good video courses on Udemy* to help you understand what body language is and how you can use it to your advantage as a real estate salesperson.

You'll need to practice actively to improve your listening skills as well. Make a commitment to yourself that you'll apply some of the tips above (and many more that you can gather on the Internet) when talking to your spouse, friends, colleagues, and relatives. Practice makes perfect. Before no time, active listening will be second nature to you. And you'll realize how much more understood your clients feel after they've had a sit down with you.

Communication Mistakes to Avoid

Recognizing bad communication habits and shedding them is an important step towards leveraging positive communication. Pay attention to your communication patterns to see if you make any of the following common mistakes that can make all the difference for landing a client on a list or buy side:

- ☐ **Arguing** – this is one surefire way to alienate your real estate prospects. If you tend to become argumentative whenever you feel like your thoughts or opinions aren't getting the response you hoped for, it's time to put a pause on this negative communication pattern. Speaking like you're arguing with prospects will only make them feel uncomfortable and uninformed. The end result? You'll lose business that you might easily have won if you had more patience and better communication.

- ☐ **Playing victim** – being a better communicator means that you have to explore your communication habits (even in your relationships and interactions with friends) and see what needs to go away. If you're the kind of person who always plays up old injuries for whatever reason, know that you're putting others in a difficult position. You want your prospects and other people around you to feel buoyed after they interact with you, not depressed. If there are mindset issues or things that happened in the past that are pulling you down, maybe it's time to finally address them, but not to your clients though.

- ☐ **Comparing yourself** – reacting to what others say by immediately relating it to something in your own life is another bad communication habit that you need to get rid of. You need to put your focus on the other person without letting distractions like these come in the way.

- ☐ **Judging** – we already said that judging what your prospects are prospects are saying is a major detriment to active listening and proper communication. People who make critical judgments about others are usually insecure about themselves. If you find yourself making negative comments in your mind, then you're falling off the bridge and missing the point altogether.

- ☐ **Gossiping** – just like judging, gossiping frequently adds no value to your communication. The best relationships (even in real estate) are based on honesty, trust, and integrity. If you find yourself retreating to gossip about this or that client, then you have a bad communication habit that needs to go away.

- ☐ **Interrupting** – interrupting your real estate prospect is perhaps the easiest way to tell them that you have zero interest in whatever they are saying. It's a clear statement that you think only your opinion and words as '*the professional*' have value. Teach yourself to be patient enough to let the other person finish speaking. You can always ask any questions (clarifying questions) when they pause.

Chapter 6:

5 Star Presentations

A major key to reaching your real estate goals is to give excellent presentations. Very few agents take the time they need to improve their presentation skills. It doesn't suit you if you spend a lot of money on marketing and lead generation only to perform dismally when it's time to present yourself to your clients. How you convey your message is just as important as the message itself.

To reach the levels of success of being a superstar agent in your town or community, put some time aside to think and educate yourself on how you can make your presentations better. Great presentations help win important listings and show off properties with maximum impact. They also help prospective buyers have more confidence that you are the agent who can help them get their dream home with the least amount of hassle. Imagine a million-dollar buyer who is relocating and buying in an area he's never lived before. You get the opportunity to meet with him once while he's in town for the first time, scoping out the scenery. How important do you think it'll be for him to leave with the conviction that you truly understand his needs and the market?

How Presentations Help...

Agents who are great at presentations are also able to convey their vision to their clients and can capitalize on that very important first contact.

To some extent, it's true that real estate decisions are made based on trust. People often buy for emotional reasons and then justify their actions with logic. People will buy (or not buy) based on how they feel about you. Do they feel like they can trust you? Successful agents work to establish themselves as a trustworthy partner, not a salesperson. You want people to feel that they can trust you to offer advice and help them out on real estate matters. Most sellers will interview several agents back to back before they decide who they want to entrust with the sale of their home. If you're using your presentation to boast about your credentials, there's a good chance you'll fail to impress. Your goal is to be seen as a professional with a personal connection. You want to provide your expertise but in a way that makes your prospects will feel welcome and comfortable. Your referral business will depend upon people liking and believing you. You want them to feel that they got all they wanted. Prepare to meet your prospects in a problem- solving, professional, and confident manner. When a personal connection has been formed, then there's a business connection.

When it comes to attracting clients or closing a sale, a great presentation could be just what you need to make the difference. Spend time to improve how you present yourself to clients. Are you projecting value so that they will feel comfortable working with you? The best agents are often those who are disciplined, committed, and focused. Being focused means you do whatever it takes to find the success you need. That includes working to polish up your presentation.

Create Your Presentation Strategy

How you present yourself, your message, and your projected value will have a major say on your performance in the marketplace. Just showing up without a strategy to guide you tends to be a disastrous approach in real estate. Remember, *"if you don't have a plan, you're planning to fail."*

Successful real estate agents have a strategy to win business. They think strategically and competitively. They have a plan before a meeting. They know who their audience is, who their potential competition is, and they carry along the necessary presentation materials.

What makes a good strategy?

Asking great questions up front and pre-qualifying before even meeting for the first time is the best way to figure out what type of situation you're putting yourself into into. Learning as much as possible about your client is an important part of making your presentation more effective. Luckily for you, there are tons of tools on the Internet such as search engines and social media that will help you gather crucial information about your prospects. Simply perform a Google search on the names of the prospects you have booked an appointment with. Take note of local or professional information available on them. Doing your research this way makes it easier to answer any questions that they may have. There's a good chance your prospects will also Google you prior to your meeting so you do not want to lose the information advantage.

Social networking sites are your '*friend*' when it comes to researching clients. Search your prospects' names on Facebook, Twitter, and other social networking platforms. Go through their profile to see what they like and share. Can you learn anything about their priorities, goals, and background? I'm always happy to know my prospect's profession before we actually meet. It helps me deal with an IT engineer differently than I'll deal with an auto salesperson.

When checking my prospect's social media profiles, I'll also check their connections. Do we have any mutual friends on Facebook? Who are their LinkedIn connections, and who do they follow on Twitter? Using these sites as tools gives a lot of valuable information on the kind of referrals the prospect could send to me as well. If there's someone we know in common (maybe a past client of mine), I'll be happy to mention them. It builds credibility that much faster and I could use the mutual friend as a sponsor. Part of being a great agent is coming up with creative ways to help create results. After all, if a seller's house isn't selling and it's priced correctly, it'll be on you to figure out some creative ways to attract more traffic, right? Another key piece is being able to communicate what you do. If you can explain your value and let the prospect figure out that they should work with you in a confident and clear manner, you'll win more business.

Prepare to win

Great real estate presentations are researched and rehearsed well in advance. Practice makes perfect, that's all you need to make your presentations great. It's common for agents to use the initial meeting to ask important questions so they can understand the prospect's needs. But you don't have to wait until the meeting to get some of this information. Be sure to ask a few questions when setting the appointment. Understanding your prospect's goals and their pain points this early will give you a lead over the competition.

During the appointment setting call, say something along the lines of "*I appreciate the chance to meet you…to make the most out of our time together, can you tell me a little about your goals in buying a home and how I can help you reach them?*"

This question will essentially help you kill two birds with the same stone. To start with, your prospect will see you as a trusted advisor and not a pushy salesperson. You are also showing that you value their time and what is important to them.

Once you know their goals, you'll be in a better position to craft a powerful presentation. During the meeting, you can make the prospect feel that you are trying to sell based on their own points of view, which gives you an advantage. So, don't wait till you meet to start gathering the crucial information.

Use visuals to tell a story

Successful agents use stories with powerful visuals to make their presentations more effective. Giving out professional materials such as brochures, flyers and postcards during marketing presentations usually works out great. Make sure that when available, these materials are reinforcing the main points of your presentations. You want to make your messaging more memorable and very clearly understood.

You do not want your materials to be thrown down the garbage can immediately after you leave. Make sure you create personal presentations with high-impact visuals. Your materials should at the very least feature your prospect's name. Attach reports with local information. These might include neighborhood reports or buyer/seller FAQs, local resources, among other things. Colorful maps, charts, and images tend to be ideal. Where possible, include a comment pointing out important information for the prospect.

Avoid making your visuals a mere pile of just facts, figures and graphics. Instead, use simple examples and tell stories that will make your data meaningful in the context of your prospect.

For agents, the number of days on market, percentage of list price and sales-to-listing ratio are everyday jargon. But these tidbits of information might be hard to understand for your prospects. So, make sure your presentation is simplified to a 7th-grade level. Educational materials are a lot more valuable than beautiful images. Special reports, tips and tricks, and anything useful is more likely to be retained even after the transaction. You'll be leaving a trail of materials that your prospect's family members and friends can see much later and contact you.

Instead of bragging (by directly talking about your achievements), show how you have helped others. Always let the testimonials do the bragging for you. A good idea would be to include a section in your presentation that includes a few of your top testimonials. Make sure to include the contact information of the people who wrote the testimonials so your prospect can call and verify them if need be.

Be proactive

I'd like to share an interesting story I read about the *'proactive'* duck. At a hotel's outside area, ducks were gathered around the tables looking for food. The birds would wait till the diners left and then they would run to the table to look for crumbs and other leftovers on the floor. There were dozens of them fighting over the scraps left behind. *And then there was this one duck.* It was different. Rather than waiting for the diners to leave, it would always show up at their table whenever the food was delivered. And then it would look up when they were just about to eat. Interestingly, every person would take something off of their plate and drop it down to feed this duck. They fed the bird BEFORE they started to eat. Think about it. This duck refused to settle for the leftovers. He always ate the best food from the plate and he didn't even have to fight with the others to get it.

This same concept can be imported to real estate prospecting and presentations. Some agents will do the basics and hope for the best. They will make a few calls here and there and hope that they'll get a client. But successful agents aren't like that. They go the whole way. They are proactive. They will diligently search for buyers of their new listing. They will answer all the questions the home buyer might have. They will offer extra tips and think outside the box. These are the ducks who are fed the chef-cooked food right from the plate. They don't wait to scramble for the leftovers.

Proactivity is a major part of the powerful real estate presentation. When we are proactive, it allows our clients to feel that we are prepared and suited to represent them. There are many ways to be proactive. You could let your buyers know about utilities that will need to be turned on or off and potential hiccups that could be in the closing. Talk to them about potential home inspection requests and everything else you think that might be handy, to help make the entire process smooth and satisfying for both parties. If your clients keep calling you, then you probably aren't giving them enough information. Proactive real estate agents are biased towards action. Rather than waiting for something to happen, they take charge and make things happen. They find and solve problems (rather than turn away whenever there's a problem), they take personal responsibility and persevere until they reach their goals.

Proactive agents will not be afraid of change and they're always looking for opportunities to empower themselves.

The power of persuasion

Successful agents make sure that their presentations are very informative and highly persuasive. They aim to provide new information with a clear objective and call to action.

Your goal when trying to close deals is to walk out of every meeting with a signed listing agreement or buyer's exclusive agency. Your presentation should aim to achieve just that. Make sure that as you go on with your presentation, you are checking your progress. *How engaged are your prospects at various stages? Are they asking questions that show how interested they are? Are they developing the trust in you they need to move forward?* Every presentation is different, but you should have a good idea of what you want to focus on so you can motivate your prospect to take action.

The call to action should particularly be very strong. It won't matter much if you deliver a great presentation but fail to gain an agreement. If you're not a very good closer, a good idea is to squeeze in '*trial closes*' as you go on with the presentations. Trial closes are questions that are designed to help gain an agreement.

For instance, I might say, "*Well, Ms. Seller, we've had a chance to get to know each other a bit, and I feel confident we can definitely get the job of selling your home done. Based on what we've done so far, are there any concerns you have as to why we wouldn't do business together?*"

If you get an agreement on minor points in the course of your presentation, it will be easier to agree on a major point later on. Persuasive speaking is all about changing or reinforcing people's attitudes, values, beliefs, and behavior. People will only respond in the way you for intend them to. Since you're dealing with people at the level of their needs, you have to focus on dealing with emotions more than facts. So, make sure you keep the emotions of your prospects in mind.

Keep at it

Most agents feel fired up and motivated when they attend a seminar or coaching session. They feel positive they can work to improve their businesses. But the hard part is actually doing what you have learned. That is what distinguishes the successful agents from agents who continue to perform at a low level.

It takes time and a lot of practice before you learn to make your presentations flawless. The better you get at it, the more effortless it's going to be. You'll find that as you work to gain experience, you'll often go '*off track*' with your goals. Don't feel demotivated if this happens to you. What's important is that you put yourself back in line. Continual reinforcement and improvement are very important.

John Wooden, the UCLA basketball head coach, had a few rules: "*don't whine, don't complain, and don't make excuses*". Even when things aren't going right, don't complain or look for something/someone to blame. Just keep moving forward.

There are over 2 million active real estate agents in this country. You're not just going to do the normal everyday stuff and hope that you'll be among the very best. You've got to go the extra mile. You've got to sweat the stuff others aren't sweating. You need discipline and commitment. Just like the best athletes who train consistently, you've got to consistently improve your business. The fact that you're already reading this book tells me that you're very interested in success. But I really want to challenge you to practically implement what you're learning.

Asking the right questions

How you ask the questions while communicating with clients is crucial. Sales masters ask powerful open-ended questions and then pay keen attention to the responses. They avoid the basic *'yes or no'* questions because there's really nothing to learn from these.

Ask questions that help you move forward when dealing with seller listings and real estate buyers. You want to make it as easy as possible for your client to state their needs and any problems they want addressed. When you phrase your questions around this, you'll be seen as a solution-oriented professional who knows what they really want.

Dealing with sellers

What questions should you ask when presenting to a seller? To start with, you already know that they want to sell…but why are they selling? Your line of questioning should be such that it helps you gather as much information as possible:

1. Mr. and Mrs. Seller, how long have you lived in this home?
2. Why are you planning to sell?
3. Where do you plan to move when you sell?
4. What updates have you made to the home since you've lived in it?
5. What advantage(s) do you feel you have on the other homes of a similar price and square footage in the neighborhood?

Notice that each of these questions are purpose-driven. They help you personalize your presentation to the needs of the prospects. When you start by asking questions like these, you are able to build credibility and focus on what your client's exact motivation is for selling their home.

"Mr. & Mrs. Seller, I appreciate you allowing me in your home and sharing with me your real estate goals. I'm confident I can get the job done of selling your home. If you don't mind, may I now tell

A little about myself and my team's approach to marketing your home?"

This question will allow you to give a little bit of information on your credentials. Make it a few sentences about how long you've lived in the area and how many families you've helped find homes in the area. You might also say a thing or two about your team's approach. Do you have a network that you can leverage to get this home sold fast? What do you do to make sure that buyers get interested in the client's home before they purchase someone's else's? Tell the client – in a clear and confident way – why you're the right agent.

Once you establish your motivations and suitability for selling, the next few questions should seek to unveil the client's expectations:

- May I ask some questions to help sell your home as quickly as possible? I'll need to take some notes, is that okay?
- If you were a buyer in today's market, what would you pay for your home in its current condition?
- As a new buyer, would you really want some things updated to fit the current market trends?

Also, ask their progress in finding a replacement home. After finding out where and when they plan to relocate once their home is sold, ask other great questions like:

- Do you feel like it'll be harder to sell your home or purchase a replacement home?
- How soon would they like to be sold and closed?

Again, these questions will help you uncover a lot about the seller's motivations and expectations. Without knowing your client's why, it can be very hard to be on the same page and live up to their expectations of hiring you. After knowing this valuable information, you can go ahead to present your solutions to their problems. Be very clear about the steps you are going to take to meet their needs.

Tell the client how you're going to list their home, at what price point range, and why. Once you engage your client with thoughtful, solution-oriented questions, you'll find that they are more willing to work with you and really find trust in moving forward with hiring you.

Dealing with Buyers

Your primary objective is to get to know your buyers. The trial and error method, where you just put clients in your car and show them dozens of homes, usually leads to wasted time and energy for both of you.

Shelter, just like food and clothing, is a basic need. People need to have a roof over their heads. A place they can call home. Your role as a real estate agent is to know what kinds of buyers are in the market so you can present better.

In any market, there's a buyer pool. These are people who are interested to buy real estate property in a certain location and at a certain price range. The buyer pool is different from spectators. They have an interest and the buying power. If you have some experience already, you'll automatically be able to distinguish between buyers and prowlers. The characteristics of the buyer pool will change from time to time. Some buyers in your pool may decide they want to buy a home elsewhere. Others may get frustrated and put their plans on hold. There are also different types of buyers in the pool:

- ☐ There are end buyers who are looking for a house they can live in.
- ☐ There are professional buyers who include other brokers, builders and investors who may be looking to develop real estate in your location. Developers usually buy strictly for the land value.

- [ ] There are cash buyers who pay in dollars and do away with the mortgage, lending and other financing options that could prolong the transaction.
- [ ] Mortgage buyers make a huge percentage of the buyer pools. A mortgage buyer can be either pre-qualified or pre-approved. Pre-qualified buyers have started the discussions with their bank. Pre-approved mortgage buyers, on the other hand, have already secured a commitment to receive a certain amount of money from the bank.

Now that you are familiar with the kinds of buyers you are likely to find in your market, the next step is to understand their perspective.

The buyer perspective

One of the reasons why successful agents sell faster is because they are able to look at a property through the buyer's eyes. Put yourself in their shoes: is there anything they might be seeing about the property in question that you haven't already noticed yourself? One trick that often helps is to go across the street and take a long, hard look. What can you see about the house that you might not have noticed before? Then go to the backyard, garage, alleys and bathrooms. Think '*out of the box*'. Can you notice anything that needs to be addressed before the home is put on the market?

Think about what they want to see in the kind of home they can't resist. The only way you'll be able to do this is by being keen. I'll usually start with the outside of the house.

- Are there any garbage cans, discarded scraps of wood, or forgotten building materials that could signal seller negligence to a potential buyer?
- Are the gutters and the roof intact? When is the last time any of these were changed?
- Are there termites, insects or other pests in the house?
- Are there overgrown tree branches around the house?

- How well does the lawn look? Is it healthy and appealing?
- Have the decks and patios been converted into storage areas? Can the buyer see what they look like?
- Is the paint already peeling off or does the house look drab and uninviting?
- Are there lights outside the house?
- What kind of location is this? How safe is the neighborhood?

These are just a few questions to guide you. Be as thorough as possible so you can understand everything about the property. You'll find it easier to answer the buyer's questions this way. You will also know to differentiate between a lead who might make a great buyer for the property, and one that might not. If the home looks dilapidated or has uninviting features, pre-renovation can make the sale much easier. Pay special attention to the clutter, color, and the cleanliness of the home. Many buyers have a pretty fixed idea of what makes a house bright, clean and uncluttered. And yet many sellers ignore these simple factors. Clutter – especially – can be a huge turnoff for buyers. It makes it harder for a buyer to mentally move into a home. They will have a difficult time imagining where they will put their sofas and other household items because clutter hampers visualization.

There's a huge difference between how you live in a home and the way you sell it. Some clutter might give a home a *lived-in* feeling. But too much of it will make it very hard for buyers to imagine the home as their own. This is a simple fact every real estate agent should keep in mind when working with seller listings. You want to do everything you can to make the home as '*sellable*' as possible before you start inviting buyers to take a look.

Also, it's important to treat all buyers with respect, whether they are inexperienced first-time buyers or professional buyers. Honesty is a serious and powerful quality on your resume. If there are environmental issues in the vicinity of the home, make sure you point it out. If lead and water poisoning issues have been reported, just be open about it.

Honesty and transparency are core values that support the real estate business. You're in this for the long haul, and you want your customers to trust you and refer you to people within their sphere of influence. Most buyers make decisions based on the full disclosure provided to them. And do I even need to say that there are legal requirements to be truthful about (such as seller property disclosures) when selling real estate?

High producing agents don't waste valuable time. They schedule an interview with the buyer(s) before embarking on the home hunt. This meeting is crucial to set the right expectations and help your client find a great home and will save you from a lot of headaches. Below are some of the key questions I'll ask my buying client during the meet-up.

What's their motivation for buying a house?
Why do they want to buy a home? Is it because they got a new job in town and have to relocate? Is it because of pregnancy or a child leaving for college so they need to downsize? This is extremely important information that will help guide you and make their house hunting successful.

What monthly mortgage payment amount are they comfortable with?
Just because a buyer can qualify for half a million dollars in mortgage doesn't mean they are willing to buy a $500,000 house. Many of your buyers already have talked to their bank and know how much they can qualify for. But they don't understand how much they need to pay in monthly mortgage servicing for a house of a certain size. It's up to you to break this down for them so you can narrow down on a home they are comfortable paying for. Another helpful tip is to make sure your clients understand what's included in their mortgage payment as far as taxes, homeowners insurance, private mortgage insurance (PMI) and any other

potential assessments. This helps to prevent sticker shock after you've put a home under contract.

Tip: In most cases, when typing an offer for your buyers, you should have an estimated cost sheet available for your buyers as well when you present them with the offer for signing. It helps if you truly understand what goes into these numbers to explain them to your clients, but you can always reach out to the loan office on the deal or to have them send you over a more accurate estimated cost sheet. The reason theirs will be more accurate is because every bank has different loan origination fees and bank fees.

What are their needs and desires in a home?
Client's needs are very important and are 'must-haves' when looking for a home. Desires are the 'wants'. Collecting this information early on will help you filter down to the right house. Often, there usually is no one-size-fits-all. So, you may have to inform your buyer that they might need to make compromises on their needs and desires. I always share with my clients the 80/20 rule. I let them know in the initial meeting to sit down and write the 5 most important features they need to feel comfortable with purchasing a new home. If they can get 4 of those 5 things, it's a home they should move forward with because there is no such thing as a perfect home.

Do they understand the costs of purchasing a home?
Again, most buyers know that they need to make a down payment when purchasing a home. But many people tend to be caught unawares by additional expenses such as option fees, home inspection, termite, earnest money, appraisal, and sometimes survey costs. It's likely that some of these fees may be credited back after closing, but you need to help the buyer familiarize with all out-of-pocket expenses involved.

The last thing you would want is for your clients to get the home of their dreams under contract and not have enough money to close. Let's say, for example, you have a FHA buyer who is buying a 200k house. They have it set in their mind that since they are first-time home buyers they only need 3.5% for their down payment ($7,000). What if they were never educated on the extra costs? When they see their initial disclosure docs from their lender, they tend to only focus on having their down payment, only to find out they actually need $13,500 and they don't have nearly enough to close on the home in the next 30-45 days. Now, the blame is pointed at you because you didn't guide them in the right direction.

Do they know that a Homeowner's Association membership may be required in some neighborhoods?

Different buyers have different opinions on Homeowner Associations. Make sure you point out areas and situations where the HOA is a must.

Will they live in the home, or is it an investment property?

Traditionally, many people buy a home so they can be build memories with their family. Nowadays, though, buyers are more economic-minded. It's common to come across buyers who are very keen on the long-term potential of their investment. You need to be well versed with the information they might be interested in. For instance, are there any good schools in the area? You can use the internet to find resources that provide such information and offer those resources to your clients in order to make the best decisions for them. Regardless of whether it's an investment property or a property they are planning to live in for years to come, make sure your clients understand the potential risk of capital gains if they sell too quickly. This is another great way to provide education and a valuable resource by connecting them with a knowledgeable professional that can offer more in-depth advice on their situation.

Are they working with a financial professional?

Buying a home being the massive transaction that it is, there are so many factors at play here. Your goal is to take charge of the entire process. I always tell my clients that it is beneficial if all their agents (real estate, CPA, and financial advisor) are on the same page. This helps to streamline the process.

How soon do they need to move, and why?

This is another important question that will help you figure out how serious the buyer is. Of course, you'll want to focus more of your energy on buyers who intend to move soon. An excellent idea is to put more long-term buyers (those who might take a few months, or even a year) on a drip campaign. This way, you'll be able to keep tabs by giving them information to prepare them when the time is ripe to buy.

Chapter 7:

Act Like You've Done it Before

The goal of this chapter is to help you get the total picture when it comes to selling real estate. It highlights some essential principles that myself and other successful agents use to be more effective when selling properties. You'll learn that you need to cultivate a certain mindset in order to succeed consistently. You want to get the whole piece of the pie, right? It takes more than luck to get it. Market conditions will improve one year and deteriorate the next. Condos will be hot one year and cold the next. Rental property will be the in-thing one season, and low-demand the next season.

Be a Professional

Buyers can easily tell whether you're a real estate agent or a real estate professional. Agents sell some homes sometimes, but full-time professionals sell a lot of homes all the time. I tell my coaching mentees that attitude is everything. A positive attitude is the number one characteristic of a real estate professional. Even when markets are not doing well, a professional will look for opportunities. But first things first, you have to look the part. Imagine that your clients were looking to hire a lawyer to represent them, and then the lawyer shows up with holy jeans and a tank top. Would they want that person representing them? Of course not. The same thing applies to you as a real estate agent. You have to cultivate an image that inspires confidence.

Do you present yourself as competent and knowledgeable?

Does your communication reflect a successful and professional real estate agent?

Do you have an organized and efficient follow-up system?

These are some of the questions you should ask yourself. Punctuality and integrity are also very important. Buying a home is one of the biggest transactions many people make in their entire lifetime. Few home sellers and buyers are going to trust this endeavor on you if you do not handle yourself like a professional. The client's comfort level in you is always very important.

There are always people in your area of focus who need professional help with real estate. But are you in tune? Are you reading the classifieds or making an effort to know what's going on? Are you networking with contractors, builders, bankers, insurance companies, trustees, brokers and other stakeholders in the real estate industry? Reach out and see people. This is one of the ways you are going to ensure you have a steady stream of leads in your business.

Negotiate from a Position of Power

Effective negotiating is crucial in closing a deal. Unlike trying to buy a car at the auto dealership, real estate negotiations can become long, complicated and tense. It's your job as an agent to advocate for your client's goals. And at the same time, you need to make the other party feel that they got a great deal too.

The most successful real estate agents negotiate from a point of power. I approach every situation with confidence because I truly believe I can come up with a win-win solution for everyone involved. If you don't display the confidence in yourself from early on, how can you expect your clients to have the confidence to hire you for the job of handling the biggest investment of their lifetime? As an agent, sometimes it's easy to get caught up in the emotional side and feel like you're making decisions for your client, but you have to remember: it's only business and your job is to pass along and guide the client as best as possible.

Negotiating tips

As a real estate agent, you should always be working to improve your negotiating skills. You should know how to come up with a plan that presents itself as a win-win scenario for both the seller or buyer. But how do you do this?

Before you start negotiating, it's good to set limits that you know up front you can stick to. For example, if you are negotiating on behalf of the buyer and you've had a conversation with your clients about the maximum they're willing to pay for a particular home (say $125,000 in this case) and you know you can go in and fight for $120,000, you have room to move to secure the home for your clients. The same goes for the seller': what is the seller's bottom dollar and what is the buyer's top dollar? What's more important? It's not always about the money. Maybe for the seller it's about closing as soon as possible so they don't have to make another mortgage payment on this particular home. When you have this kind of information, you'll find it easier to find a reasonable compromise for everyone involved.

There's a popular negotiating quote that goes something like this, *"If you want a kitten, start out by asking for a horse."*

. In your initial offer, never narrow it down to only the things your clients truly care about, depending on the type of market you're in Let's say the seller does some cosmetic work, such as painting, and you know that your clients could handle doing it themselves, but by having this in the negotiations, it gives you cushion to remove at a later time and gain leverage as being willing to compromise. This gives them something to say no to, and you might end up with a better deal. In a buyer's market, the biggest negotiating mistake you can make is to start with your best offer and have no leverage for your clients on the backend.

If you're dealing with first-time buyers or sellers, understand that they might feel a little apprehensive about the transaction. It's their first time buying a home. This is most likely the biggest transaction they've ever made. You need to respect their feelings and do as much as you can to demystify the process for them. Set the right expectations, give them an outline, a timetable, and be proactive with anything else you can offer to show them what to expect as the transaction goes forward.

Representing a seller

- *Create a sense of urgency* – when a buyer comes knocking, it's important that you give them a response that will motivate them to act quickly. You want to let them know if you've received any other offers or notice an offer coming in from other potential buyers but be careful not to scare them away. Many buyers are not interested in a bidding war and may run away at the smell of one.
- *Set the limits* – as mentioned earlier, it's important to get to the seller and buyer limits so you can negotiate a sensible deal. What is the buyer's top dollar, and what is the seller's bottom dollar? If the buyer makes a considerably low initial offer, counter with small amounts to see how much they'll increase before they state that what they offered is the highest they can go.
- *Provide a concession free counter option* – mentioning closing costs, home warranties, and title insurance premiums can help soften the buyer's stance. I might say something like, "$200,000 sales price. Seller agrees to pay
$4000 towards closing costs. $500 towards a home warranty. The alternative to this is $195,500 sales price. No concessions."

Representing the buyer

- *Get more info from the listing agent* – when representing a real estate buyer, a major step will be to talk to the listing agent and ask a few questions. Are there other offers on the table right now? Can the seller accommodate a quick closing? Has the seller received any offers that they rejected? Often, this should give you some valuable information to help craft a decent offer of your own.

- ☐ *Get to the seller's bottom price* – the goal is to get to the seller's lowest possible price before you even mention the buyer's highest offer. You can then let your buyer decide whether they're willing to go with this price. If so, you can engage the listing agent in counter-offers till you get the best possible deal.
- ☐ *Offer higher, counter less* – it's common that some buyer agents like to start very low with plans to go up significantly if need be. Practically, though, the negotiation works much better when you make an offer that's higher and make each counter less.
- ☐ *let the other party sign off on the final terms first* – you do not want to submit your final say first only for the opposing agent to spend the next 24 hours shopping for a better deal…all the while sitting on your signed terms. When you request the other party to sign off first, you essentially give your client the final say.

Selling Skills = Relationship Skills

There's a very thin line between sales skills and relationship skills. In the past, the idea of the salesperson was that pushy, loudmouthed guy who was seen as nagging and aggressive. But most industries have gotten beyond that image. Top movers and shakers use everyday relationship skills to secure new business.

Being a good real estate salesperson starts with telling everyone in your circle what you do for a living. Start with your neighbors, dentist, people at your church, store clerks, and everyone you come across. Make sure they know you're a real estate agent. The problem many new real estate agents suffer with is they don't let enough people know they're in the business. If you're a secret agent, no one can do business with you because they don't know who you are. Every day, you must focus on letting your community know you're the go-to agent for all things real estate. There are no excuses nowadays for not building your brand daily since social media and cell phones are with you 98% percent of the day.

It's easy to see how selling skills are so similar to relationship skills. When you want somebody to do something, you've got to show them that it's to their advantage, that they can benefit from it. It's all about solving problems in a mutually beneficial way. More importantly, you have to have credibility so your clients know, like, and trust you. If you present a solution to them, human nature is to be skeptical up front. Then they'll go through the decision-making process and ask themselves if you're credible enough and whether or not they trust you. Continuously branding yourself as the expert in the community is how you'll get more credibility, build faster relationships, and ultimately convert more prospects into clients.

But you don't have enough time to build a relationship with everyone you meet, right? That's why you should focus on the decision makers. You don't want to waste all your energy talking to someone who can only tell you no, but can't tell you yes. Be careful though, because, on the other hand, you also don't want to ignore the decision influencers. These are the support people around the decision maker who influence the decision. For instance, if a young couple is looking for a home and you know one of their parents, make sure that, if they accompany you on the listing presentation, showing, or even home inspection walk through, you recognize and address their concerns as well. They could help influence the decision to have you as the official agent.

Here are a few relationship-building tips that work:

Communicate often – selling a home isn't as easy as selling a car. There won't be new developments every day. But that doesn't mean that you should stop touching base with your clients. You might be doing a lot of work behind the scenes to get the home your clients are looking for, but they won't know unless you can explain it to them in a language they can understand.

Also, ask up front how your clients would like to be communicated with and set the right expectations. If your clients know you start your family time at 8PM, they will be apprehensive to give you a call that late unless it's an emergency. In today's world as well, many of your clients will prefer to text: this can be good or bad, but just remember there's a lot of emotion going into each transaction, so things can be misinterpreted sometimes through text. So a phone call will always be the lead option. If text is the preferred method and there's multiple decision makers in the process, set up a group text to ensure all parties are on the same page. Great relationships are powered by regular communications. Be transparent and proactive. Your leads should feel that you are available whenever they have something to discuss, but if you don't set the right expectations, you can find yourself with disgruntled clients who feel like you over promised and under delivered.

Honesty is key – if you're a successful agent, you already know that honesty is a priceless quality. If you promise something to your clients, be accountable, follow through and make sure you deliver. If there are issues that pop up along the way, be honest with your clients and find alternative ways to accomplish a solution and get the deal to closing. There will always be something new to learn in real estate, set the right expectations up front, and let your clients know there being over 25 people that will touch your clients file throughout the transaction (title, loan officer, processors, admin, etc.), there's no way you can prevent every hiccup that could pose a block in the deal, but with communication from everyone, you'll get through it in the end. Transparency can go a long way into building the kind of relationships you will need in your business. Don't promise anything if you know you can't get it done. There's no need to try to be a miracle worker. What your clients truly want to know is that no matter what issues arise, you'll be there to assist them and find a solution.

Paint yourself as a trusted advisor and resource – the more value you offer, the stronger your relationships will be. People are more than eager to recommend an agent who goes above and beyond. To be a valuable resource, make sure you have all the pertinent information at your fingertips. Some things to consider in order to stay atop of your game:

- Do you know how the local market is doing?
- Can you advise a client on when the best time to sell is?
- Are you reading articles and reports that expand your knowledge so you can help your buyers and sellers much better?
- Do you know a local handyman to help them with repairs before going to market?
- Do you have a good recommendation on a home inspection company to help them be prepared for any requests the buyers might ask for?

People will easily tell between an agent who knows their turf and one who's struggling.

Think of your clients as more – to build better relationships in your real estate business, think of your clients as more than just a means of generating income. Treat each client as an individual and take note of their concerns and interests. The more you can identify with your prospects as a person, the stronger the bond will be.

Reward your loyal clients – don't make the mistake of taking your clients who've already done business with you for granted. It's common that business owners – not only in the real estate world – become so fixated on acquiring new business that they forget their existing clients. There's no point working so hard to build relationships only to ignore your clients who already know, like, and trust you. Make sure that you reward your best clients with exclusive discounts, rewards, and anything else.

Here's a cool tip: let's say you come across concert tickets that you aren't necessarily interested in or can't attend. Instead of turning them down, grab them and reach out to your top A-list clients and offer them over. Regardless of whether they're interested in the tickets or not, they will love the fact you reached out to them to try to offer something out of kindness. These are the types of gestures that will get you more referrals. Often, even personalized holiday cards can do the trick. Anything you can do to say, *'thank you for allowing me to be your go-to for all things Real Estate.'*

Provide resources to your clients – Often, when someone is buying or selling their home, they don't have all the resources to make it a seamless and easy process up front. Providing resources to your clients is a great way to strengthen your relationships with them. By providing resources that are useful or interesting, you prove your worth as a real estate agent. Some of the relationships I would recommend you set out to create from day one are connections such as:

- Home stager
- Home inspector
- Mortgage loan officer
- Landscaper
- Roofer
- Handyman
- Title companies (can help with FSBO as well)
- Real estate attorneys

A blog will go a long way too. You can share information on local real estate, schools, and anything else they might be interested in. With real estate becoming more nationalized, you could be contacted by someone looking to move into your community and they've been following your blog for quite some time so you already have credibility with them. You can also have your clients subscribe to your blog so they can receive a notification whenever you share something. This is a great way to keep your name and brand name in their mind.

Think long-term - building relationships in your real estate business is a long-term effort, and you'll do better when you think of it that way. It's a marathon, not a sprint. Again, remember the prosecuting you do today is for 30, 60, even 120 days from now. It takes a lot of time to build strong, valuable relationships. If you start thinking of it as a short-term effort, you'll be disappointed. Use your communication skills to influence others so they can see you as a helpful, resourceful agent.

Dealing with upset real estate prospects

You'll probably have dealt with a few angry, emotional or upset clients in your real estate career. It happens. But how do you handle the situation with professionalism? It's easier than you might think. The worst reaction you can have to an upset client situation is to get upset yourself. You want to let the client know that everything is in control and that you're ready to provide the solution that will address whatever problem is at hand.

What if a buyer who recently bought a home through you discovers that a new roof will be needed? They might become very angry at the home seller and perhaps even you for not disclosing the roof issue. Even though this might not have been your fault, you still have to remain cool, calm, and collected. Below are a few techniques I use to ease the situation whenever one of my clients is upset or emotional for whatever reason.

a) Listen

Listening should be your biggest priority whenever you have a difficult client. Simply let them talk it out without interrupting. This will allow them to get their concerns off their chest and see that you care to listen. The next step will be to determine the sources of their woes.

Anger is usually just a symptom. There ought to be something which is driving it. It might be as a result of fear. Maybe the buyer is afraid they might not be able to install a new roof because they have already spent a lot of money. Maybe they are afraid their financial plan and move-in budget will scatter. The buyer could also be wondering what other problems the seller may have concealed since they didn't mention the roof issue. It's important you find the true issue beneath the anger. The best way to do this is to remain calm and ask good questions.

Only after you identify the real issue will you be able to deal with it. A lot of times people will get upset because things turn out differently than they didn't expect it. They might also feel like they have no control over the process, or maybe they are not feeling respected. You might have to deal with buyers who really are not committed to buying a home despite going through with the process. Whatever the issue is, make sure to ask questions and truly listen to get to the bottom of it.

b) Find a solution

After you understand the client's woes, the next step is to find a solution that really works. Put yourself in their shoes and imagine what you would do. Show the client that you are on their side and that you're going to do whatever you can to help them. This will be very important in order to maintain a valuable relationship in the future. People won't forget it if they see you are willing to go above and beyond to offer an excellent service.

c) Make sure your client's expectations are in line

To avoid run-ins with upset clients, work extra hard to make sure their expectations are in line from the beginning. You can start doing this by making sure you do not overpromise and under deliver. When representing a seller, never guarantee you can sell their home for X amount of money. I would always let my clients know no one can predict what your home will sell for besides the market. Another useful tip is to make sure your potential sellers know there's only three reasons a home won't sell. 1.) Price 2.) Condition 3.) Location. If the home is in a great location and the price is fair for the market, I would recommend taking a hard look at the condition the home is in. There's no point of overpromising for the purpose of making the sale or taking a listing. You might score one client but then you'll lose an opportunity to forge the kind of relationships winning real estate agents rely on all the time.

If your client is upset because they mistakenly think you misled them, bring them closer to reality. Use your personal experience, knowledge of the community, marketing statistics and insights, or whatever else you can to make them see the picture clearly.

d) Keep emotions under control

People tend to get unsettled when they feel like a specific situation is spiraling out of control. This is even truer when real estate is involved. Use your good communication skills to make sure this does not happen. Even the most basic things about real estate might be new to your clients. Keep in mind you're the real estate expert, not them. So, make it a point to explain things every step of the way. Let them know what they can expect and what they can do to help (if anything). It's your job to keep your clients in the loop.

e) Show them respect

Showing disrespect is like putting a noose around your relationship. But often, people feel disrespected because of the smallest things. Maybe you're bombing them with real estate jargon they can't understand and they feel like they are being left out of their own transaction, or even feel like you're not really negotiating the best deal on their behalf. It's also possible that you might be feeling a little burnt out and have less energy to handle difficult clients. So, your actions tend to be interpreted as disrespect. If you're feeling exhausted, take a little break and then come back once you have rested. Remember, real estate in general, especially residential, is an emotional purchase. The key is to remain CCC: Cool, Calm, and Collected.

Operating with integrity

Integrity will go a long way to distinguish yourself from other real estate agents. Few things are as important in relationship building as trust. You might be very knowledgeable and skilled. You might have a very vibrant team of capable assistants. You might even build a high-value network of referral resources. But without trust, your business is like a house that's been built on a shaky foundation.

It takes time to get clients to trust you, especially if you just started out as a real estate agent. You're going to need a consistent pattern of honesty, quality and service in order to be seen as trustworthy. Always be upfront and truthful about your intentions. Maintaining an open line of communication is also important in order to build trust and nurture your relationships. Make sure you share information and encourage feedback. This way, you'll be able to know the concerns your clients have so you can address them.

Another important part of operating with integrity is to admit when you make a mistake. We are all human. We are bound to make errors here and there. But when we do, the honorable thing to do is acknowledge and fix it.

Never over promise and under deliver just to soothe your ego. Fulfill your promises and your clients will see you as trustworthy and deserving of respect. Work extra hard to give people more than they expect and they'll be even more willing to refer you.

When the stakes are high, your integrity should be even higher. Don't be tempted to move into a gray area because you think it will net you with more profits. Focus on delivering an excellent service as your business's priority. Warren Buffett, Chairman and CEO of Berkshire Hathaway, said it best: "In looking for people to hire, look for three qualities: integrity, intelligence, and energy. And if they don't have the first one, the other two will kill you." When you build your business on the solid foundation that is trust and integrity, it'll grow and flourish.

Understanding Key Financing Options

When it comes to lending money, financial institutions (banks and mortgage lenders) usually have a set criteria – or profiles – for individuals they are happy to lend money to. These requirements may be at least a credit score of 620 or a 55 max DTI (Debt To Income) ratio. These numbers factor into how they will structure a loan that's in their own best interest, and it's up to you to do your homework whether you're working as an agent or investor. A lot of the times if you have a solid relationship with a MLO (Mortgage Loan Officer) or banker, you can get them to look harder at a deal because they know you have credibility. This is one of the reasons why relationships are golden in real estate. Below, I've put together some of the key financing options you might want to familiarize yourself with:

→ **Construction/Permanent loans**

This is one way to finance a real estate purchase. A construction loan typically constitutes two loans. One that allows borrowers to buy materials for building a house. Once the building is completed, another loan is issued that is converted into a typical permanent loan. The borrower and the bank have to agree on an amount before any money is released by the bank.

Let's assume you need to borrow $200,000. After closing, you'll need part of the money to purchase the land. The bank will then release the necessary funds. Then you'll need to buy construction materials and the money will be available to you. The number of withdrawals you make will vary from one institution to the other. Once the home is built, you withdraw the final amount so you can pay the rest of the bills. This final amount you use in your project –

let's say $150,000 out of the stated $200,000 – can be converted into a permanent loan.

Construction loans tend to be interest-only loans. You'll receive a monthly bill for interest on the outstanding balance.

When it comes to buying new construction, there's a misconception that the process is pretty straightforward. Simply walk into the builder's office, pick a lot, sign some documents, and that's it! By following this approach, the buyer will be at the mercy of the builder's salesperson. Work with new construction to help your buyers make sound decisions. As an agent, it'll be your responsibility to ensure the buyer hires the right builder and to guide them on the lot, location, and neighborhood. This can be a great opportunity for you to also increase your network within the industry.

→ **Permanent (fixed rate) mortgage loans**

Major key: There are various types of mortgage loans available to buyers. The most common ones you will come across include:
- Conventional loans (which can require as little as 3% down)
- VA loans for veterans (doesn't require any money down)
- FHA loans that insure the lender from risk (commonly used for first-time home buyers – requires 3.5% down)

→ **Seller financing**

This is another type of financing that sometimes works out in real estate transactions. Seller financing involves the seller lending money to the buyer so the buyer can acquire the property in question. When the seller and the buyer agree on the logistics, this kind of financing can be wonderful for both parties. The advantage of this option for your buyers is that it leads to easy and quick loan approvals, competitive interest rates, and lower fees than banks and other institutions normally charge. The advantage to the seller is that the equity from the home turns into a source of steady income and cash flow with a much higher rate of return on their money. The loan is also secured by an asset – the house. Perhaps the only disadvantage is that if the buyer defaults on the payments, the seller would need to use legal action to get either the money or the house back seeing as they're acting as the bank. The main thing to keep in mind here is to make sure that if you are acting as an agent, you have a buyer's exclusive agency signed and it is stated in the contract exactly how the commission will be paid to you so there is no confusion.

Chapter 8:

Promoting Your Real Estate Business Online

We can all agree that real estate is huge on the Internet. Thanks to technology uptake, a lot of people spend a significant amount of their time online. Research shows that up to 80% of consumers conduct an online search before purchasing a product. And things are not so different when it comes to real estate. A lot of home sellers and buyers will start their search for an agent online, whether that be Facebook, Zillow, or even LinkedIn. Millions of homes sold every year are marketed via the Internet.

Real estate agents can no longer afford to ignore Internet marketing or to just create a simple website and call it their online strategy.

How do you structure your business online so that you get the best results?
Having a website and marketing on the Internet are two very different things. A website is more or less the same thing as having a flyer. The flyer offers important information about your business, but as long as you have it sitting on your desk, it's not adding any value to your business. You need to get it distributed out there so the people you're interested in – prospects – can read it.

In the same way, you just don't distribute your flyers to everyone. It'd be a waste of time and resources. You have to identify your target audience first. Having a website is great, but it's going to be meaningless if no one knows about it. In this chapter, I'll highlight the basics of creating an online marketing plan that actually works.

Define Your Objectives

A good online marketing plan should start with well-defined objectives. What do you want to accomplish with online marketing? Brainstorm with your team and come up with very good primary and secondary objectives. This way, you're going to be able to create a presence that helps reach your goals.

Selling your services online is usually the online marketing objective for most agents. Many people begin the process of buying or selling a home online. The NAR says that 68% of all buyers find their home online. After finding a home that really interests them, people will then contact a real estate representative. By making sure your information is visible and consistent across all platforms online, you'll make it easier for buyers to choose you and your company.

Another common website marketing objective for real estate agents is to ***provide customer support***. A website gives you a channel where your customers can get in touch with you 24/7. You might include features to schedule viewings or even offer virtual tours on some of your listings. You might also provide answers to questions (FAQs) most of the buyers or sellers in your area of focus are asking. People will value your brand if they find your information helpful and convenient.

Your website should help to ***provide information about your listings*** and locations. You want prospective buyers to see where available homes are located. You might also provide a little bit of information (related to safety, education, etc.) on each of the neighborhoods you focus on. Then when people are browsing through a home in that neighborhood, you can offer them a link where they can access this valuable information.

Promoting brand awareness should be a major goal for your online marketing plan. The Internet makes it super-easy to increase brand awareness. You want to make sure that you have a consistent brand identity across all platforms. You want to create an appealing and unique brand identity that people can remember. Once you do this, you'll be able to use sharable content to publicize your brand. *Creating a really funny animated video that people are going to share could turn out to be a phenomenal strategy as long as you're aware of who your target audience is.*

People don't buy or sell homes every other day. For that reason, ***your real estate website should be designed to encourage visitors and clients to return again and again***. It's possible that someone starts browsing homes through Google because they are planning to buy a home towards the end of the year. You want to entice them to keep coming back till they are ready for the transaction. But how do you accomplish that? Have sections where you publish featured properties every week, calendars of events, and open house invitations among other things. If someone knows they might find something interesting every time they go onto your website, then they'll be more willing to come back. But if you're offering your visitors the same page (with the same information) all year-round, they'll probably have no reason to come back. It's important that your website has sharing features. If a visitor sees a fantastic home (even if they are not ready to buy yet), they might feel compelled to share the home images with their friends on Facebook and other social media networks. You'll be getting free publicity and increased brand awareness every time someone shares something interesting on your site.

Define a Target Market

Defining a target market for online marketing efforts is just as important as listing your objectives. Without a target audience, you might do a lot of work and still attract zero results. Successful real estate agents operate with precision. If they're going to spend $100 on online marketing, they know that this money is going to make sure their content is seen by the right people. You need to determine the needs, wants, and expectations for each one of your target market segments. Possible segments for buyers might include *young families, retirees, a waterfront property, acreages, luxury homes, investment properties*, etc.

Find the '*WOW*' factor for each of these segments.
What can I offer them that will 'WOW' them? How can I exceed their expectations? The only way you'll able to answer each of these questions is by first outlining the needs, wants and expectations for each of your target market segments.

Competitor Analysis

Now that you've clearly defined your objectives, your target market, and know what services and products you are going to be offering, it's time to take a long look at your competition.

Your online competition is not the same as your offline competition. There are no boundaries online. So, your business will be competing with all sorts of organizations. This includes national real estate agencies and anyone who's offering the same products and services as you are. A thorough competitor analysis will help you figure who your toughest competition is. This way, you can learn from what they are doing and actually aim to do better yourself. There are various ways to identify competitors online. You might start by conducting a simple search, using search terms that your prospects might use. The goal is to see what websites rank highest on search engines.

Once you've gathered a list of top competitor websites, the next step is to review them element by element. Here are a couple of things you'll want to check out:

- What features your competitors are using online?
- What types of content are they feeding their audiences?
- How easy are their websites to use?

Collect every piece of information that you think can be useful.. This information will help you figure out what elements need to be included on your own website so you can position to win. This kind of reverse-engineered competitor analysis can be very instrumental to help you develop a high-value website to stay on top of the digital space for keywords in your market.

Rethink Your Website Presence

Once you figure out what features you want to include on your website (from the competitor analysis), the next step is to create a content blueprint for your site! Great websites are often so because the owners spent adequate time in the planning stage. Once you integrate your objectives, target market description, and competitor information, you'll be able to form the basis of an excellent online presence.

I get it. You probably don't have enough time to create the website content yourself. But nobody else knows your business and your target audience as well as you do. That's why it's better for you to work on the first content draft for each page. You may consider tasking one of your team members (or hiring someone like a VA) to polish up the messaging much later. By creating the first draft of the content yourself, you'll be able to align the messaging that you know works for your clients.

Your contact information should be very easy to find on your website. Consider having an individual *'Contact Us'* page that shows your office location on the map and provides multiple means to get in touch with you or one of your team members. People shouldn't struggle before they find your phone number or other contact information on your site.

On a good real estate website, the navigation and user interface should be prioritized over almost everything else. Do you want prospective buyers to see listings? Make sure they don't have to struggle to find the *'Listings'* option on your site. If you are offering video tours on the website, make sure you have a very prominent button linking to that section on your website. Also, ensure that your real estate website is as professional as possible. Just like people judge you within the first few seconds of meeting you, first impressions also matter on the Internet.

Leveraging Systems (People and Technology)

Robert Kiyosaki, while explaining the The Cashflow Quadrant, says a sentence that'll stay with you, "It's not money that makes you rich it's your business skills."

I very much believe in his theory and would like to share that with you, because I believe it will help you on your journey of becoming building your foundation in real estate.

Imagine a box with four sections inside. The upper left side is the E: for employee. The lower left side is the S: for self-employed people or for small business owners. Moving on to the right upper side, it's the B: for big business owner. And lastly, the right lower side is the I: for Investors.

Here's the thing: you can be in each corner, it's up to you.

Let's get into the details. So, as an employee, you have a job: the majority of our population is in this side. Here you basically trade your time for money, working about 30-80 hours weekly for a fixed salary. If you're a teacher, a banker, even a pilot or a nurse, then you're currently the E. The interesting thing is you can identify these people with only knowing their core values and even by knowing the words they use.

These types of people need security and that's why they go looking for safe and secured job with benefits. A lot of us start off as an employee, one huge disadvantage is you pay as much in taxes as you earn: the more you earn the more you pay in taxes. And when you stop working your salary follows your steps: it also stops. Huge problem.

Then, there are the self-employed people or the small business owners. Here, you own a job: real estate agents, doctors, lawyers, accountants and insurance agents, graphic designers and photographers, and, of course, small business owners. These people might think that they got out of the category where you trade your time for money. But that's just a lie you tell yourself: you might even have to work harder and longer. And here this: you don't even have paid vacations. When you stop working for a while, your income drastically drops and then stops.

There's a great sentence that identifies people in the S category: if you want it done right, do it yourself. Most real estate agents start out from the left side of the quadrant: being an employee, then becoming small business owners. And the real question here is how you can move to the right side of the cashflow quadrant?

For all small business owners, the good news is that it's just the beginning: most big businesses start off as self-employed, right? What they do next is put in a system that works for them and gather a strong team. That's when they have to chance to become "big."

Moving on the right side of the quadrant, there are the big business owners. If you're wondering what counts as a big business here's a clarification for you: big businesses have 500+ employees. Big business owners are always looking for a great System, a good Network, and bring the smartest people into their team: all of this helps them run their business. Ultimately, there comes a time, when a big business owner doesn't have to work, and that does not harm the business: it can still operate perfectly. I'm sure you've heard of a large mega team inside of your brokerage or even maybe on one. These teams normally have a leader that's put a system in place to leverage (OPT) other people's time.

So, as a big business owner, you want your people to work hard for you and your company. Here's something incredible: big business owners pay the least in taxes. This might sound a bit unfair, but that's the world we're living in. Moreover, even when you're sleeping or vacationing, your business still generates a cash flow for you because your system is still operating.

When you hear someone say, "Let's have a System in place and gather the best possible Team," that's when you know they've got the mindset of a big business owner. By now you probably understood that "System" and "Team" are the two main elements if you want to make your transition from a small business owner to a big business owner.

Don't get me wrong, big business owners still have to work hard for a couple of years until the system starts to work and the right people start to gather around. But after all of that, they can earn passive income that will potentially flow to them for the rest of their lives.

And the part you were waiting for the most, Investors. Robert Kiyosaki identifies them as people who have their money work hard for them. And this is everyone's end goal, right?

Investors pay less taxes than employees and small business owners and, with time, their assets start to produce cash flows for them. Their presence doesn't even count.

Marketing Automation with Tech Tools

In today's online-first marketplace, successful real estate agents make an effort to be tech-enabled. The competition is working around the clock to capture the same business that you're looking for. For that reason, you have to make sure you're always working on a comprehensive digital strategy that includes organic website optimization and pay- per- click advertising, among other online techniques.

The 2017 National Association of Realtors report states that 99% of Millennials search for real estate online, compared to 89% of Older Boomers and 77% of the Silent Generation. This, in fact, shows just how vital social media, blogging, and email marketing is to your digital marketing strategy. Your goal is to reach a bigger audience and attract more leads to your real estate business. With marketing automation tools, you can maximize your lead generation. Top agents use marketing automation to ease repetitive tasks and generally abstract the process of gathering leads. Remember: you are a small business owner. You should invest in a good computer and, if you can, find some inexpensive software programs such as *Top Producer*, *Realty Juggler, MailChimp,* and other automation tools that will help to take some of the mundane tasks off your plate.

Basically, marketing automation is all about synchronizing your real estate marketing efforts using softwares that makes publishing, sharing, and analyzing your content abstract. Rather than having to manually share every tweet, send each email and publish every blog post, marketing automation software provides an organized system that completes each of these tasks for you. It's all about distributing your real estate inbound marketing tasks with more ease.

Here are the main benefits of real estate marketing automation:

- ☐ **Lead nurturing** – automation tools let you know how far along your leads are in the sales funnel, and even recommend the next steps to continue nurturing them.
- ☐ **Real-time updates** – with real-time updates, you're alerted whenever your leads take an action. This allows you to respond in a timely manner so you can increase

engagement and let your leads know that they have your attention. Real estate agents are able to maximize the opportunity by promptly acting on communication from leads.

❏ **Save money** – rather than hiring multiple employees (or numerous software solutions) to keep your marketing and sales efforts organized, automation provides an all-in-one alternative. This way, you are able to keep everything in one place as well as reduce expenditure.

Automation doesn't replace your attention

Many real estate agents make the mistake of thinking that once they purchase a marketing automation software solution, they can finally sit back and relax. This is not the case. You still have to produce the marketing collateral…write those blog posts, create and stay on top of that drip campaign, and manage your social media posts. This is why leveraging someone on your team to handle this can be so fundamental. If your budget is not there because you're just starting out, this will be something you must set aside some time for. Particularly, real estate blogging requires plenty of your attention. A great blog can be vital to the success of your real estate website. It's important that you churn out high-quality blog posts that you can then share via automation. However good of an automation solution you have, your marketing won't be able to generate many leads if your content is not good enough.

Major key: You can use sites like Later.com, Hootsuite, or Buffer to schedule timely, automatic posts to your social media site.

When it comes to choosing real estate marketing automation tools, agents are spoilt of choice. There are dozens of vendors offering a massive variety of automation software programs.
Here are a few tips to make sure you select the best automation tool for your needs:
- Look for software with capabilities that align with your marketing strategy.

- Choose software that supports all marketing channels (website, email, social media, etc.) that you intend to use to reach leads.
- Consider how well the software integrates with other tools you may be using, such as your CRM of choice and even your mobile devices.
- Examine what support is offered for the particular automation tool in case you get stuck along the way.
- Look for a tool that is easy enough for you to grasp. There's no need to pay for complex features that you'll never use.
- Most real estate agents find more satisfaction in real-estate-industry-specific automation tools. Keep that in mind before you make your final decision.

Keep Your Visitors Coming Back

Your real estate website should be positioned to keep people coming back. You need to be able to use available tools to encourage visitors to return again and again. The reasoning here is that the more people visit your website, the more likely it is that they will find a property they are interested in and the more familiar your brand and services will be to them. Get the point?

Organizing a periodic contest for potential buyers on your website would work out great. You can promise a decent gift to whoever wins. The contest itself should be a few questions in an area that is relevant to your audience. You could offer a juicer or toast maker as the prize and that would be fine. Just anything thoughtful that your target audience would consider valuable. Simply ask people to fill an electronic ballot to enter into the contest. This way, you'll be able to collect useful information on your leads, and do it more easily.

If website visitors know that there's a quarterly contest going on through your website where they could win a free iPad or tickets to an event, they'll want to check back.

A ***"What's New" page*** is another excellent hack to get people checking back. What this page does is make it very easy for people to find the information you shared recently. The section could offer the latest listings in your area of focus, as well as useful reports or local news. If you received some award for doing an exemplary job, or helped a client land a great property, that would be a good material to include. If you added a mortgage calculator or some other feature on your website, make sure you also include that too.

Giving free stuff is an excellent way to increase traffic to your website. People love free things. So, if you can offer something that's valuable and free of charge on your website, this will be a great way to attract traffic. A mortgage calculator would be an excellent freebie. You may also compile annual real estate reports that are specific to your area and that are designed to suit the needs of your target market. For instance, I would compile a *"2018 Real Estate Trends in Neighborhood X"*. The important thing here is to make it useful. Then create a press release and share it with the local media. The media is always looking for something interesting to publish. If your report is really well-researched and features interesting information, don't be surprised if they share it and quote you. Once you grow your real estate business, you might even be able to organize an event where you're releasing a specific report and invite the local media. Freebies like this provide an ideal viral marketing opportunity for you.

Another great idea to keep your website visitors coming back is by ***partnering with local non-competing businesses*** so you can offer coupons and discounts to your audience. Think about cleaning or moving companies. You can have a small section on your website where such discounts are highlighted. As long as you are sharing legit coupons and discounts, people will be more than willing to check back. Local homeowners will be happy to come and check whether there's a new discount from cleaning companies in the area.

A **comprehensive and current calendar of open houses** will additionally keep visitors streaming to your website every now and then. Create a specific page where you only highlight open house dates. Optimize this page for search engine rankings so that your target audience can easily find it. When people are looking to purchase a property in a specific area, they usually want to know when the open houses are being held. They will be very interested in what's going on in the area. As long as you keep your calendar current and complete, you'll be sure to attract traffic. Consider using a little bit of permission marketing by asking people to leave their email address so you can notify them whenever there's an update to your calendar.

And let's not forget about having a **blog section in your website**. If you want the right people to find your site organically you have to have a blog: that's the easiest and best way of making sure your website ranks well on search engines. When you write relevant and insightful blog posts that are SEO-friendly you can basically guarantee the right traffic to your website. Let's say you wrote a blog post on the topic of "How to find the best real estate agent in Chicago." A person looking for a real estate agent in Chicago will search for you in Google and find you. If your blog post gives them valuable information, and that person decides to check you out, assuming you look trustworthy in your website, you'll get yourself a new client.

Major key: *Again, the more a visitor comes to your website, the more your brand is reinforced.* The more your target audience feels that they are part of a community, the more people will be open to doing business with you. Remember, we said that trust is a major determinant when people decide who they want to work with. If people like and trust your brand, they'll be happy to recommend you to people within their own sphere of influence.

Make the Best out of Permission-Based Marketing

Permission-based marketing is not intrusive because people volunteer to receive information from you. Once they give you their email address, you'll be able to maximize your marketing by including promotional opportunities in your newsletter or whatever other resource you are sending. You could also ask people to check something new on your website. Permission-based marketing is a great way to curve a niche for yourself and keep ahead of the competition.

Permission-based marketing form

Your permission-based marketing form (*where you ask people to provide their email so you can send them info*) should be really good. Make it simple and direct to the point. Personalize the text in the form to make it as engaging as possible. Sell the '*benefits*', not the '*features*'. Yes. There's a big difference between features and benefits. Features are the surface elements of a product, such as the listings or home tours section on your website. On the other hand, benefits show the end result of what a product can accomplish. People are interested in the benefits, not the features. *How are they going to benefit when they give you permission to send them stuff? Are they going to learn more about how they can buy their next home? Will you make it easier for them to sell their current home?* Think along these lines. People are bombarded with junk email all the time. For that reason, they need to be convinced you'll give them value, not junk. Then, they'll subscribe to or join your communication. They need to be sold on what's in it for them.

"*Join our e-club to receive member only updates and mortgage rate alerts from our preferred lenders, special seasonal updates, local coupons, information on foreclosures, and just listed/just solds in the area*"

"*Receive instant email notifications from me when properties meeting your search criteria come onto the market!*"

You can spice up your permission-based marketing by promising to offer an instant e-gift to new members, but the goal must be to **give value to your database**. If you're targeting people who might be thinking about selling their home sometime soon, you may offer a *"Special Sellers' Guide to Get the Most Out of Your Home"*.

If your marketing is done well, it gives you serious leverage over your competition. Once you get ahead of the pack, you want to stay there. How do you do this? By maximizing communication with your database. Make sure you're constantly feeding your subscribers with valuable information. You want them to keep looking forward to your content because it's really just that good.

Try Video Marketing

As we all know, fun videos are perhaps the best way to leverage the power of marketing and building a brand. People love video content. A good video is also very easy to share with others via social media or email. The Metro Trains viral marketing campaign was video-based, and it spread through social media quickly. Dropbox, too, had a very intuitive video that explained how the platform worked and helped the company onboard new customers. Video marketing can be an excellent way for real estate agents to demonstrate their expertise in the industry, engage, educate, and attract new leads. There are unlimited ways in which you can use video to market your real estate business. You can share an agent profile video, client testimonials, real estate infomercials, market updates, neighborhood tours, and informative tips. Distribute your videos through YouTube, Vimeo, Facebook, Instagram, Twitter, LinkedIn, and any other channel that you utilize for your real estate marketing. Not only is video a powerful tool to help you increase brand awareness, but it also boosts your SEO and gives you a better medium to interact with prospects. Even better, gone are the days when you had to spend thousands of dollars to create high-quality videos. There are dozens of affordable, easy-to-use apps that you can utilize to create great video content. These services include Covideo, Bomb Bomb, Renderforest and more.

A well-done video will do wonders for your brand name. It doesn't have to be a real-estate specific video. It can be anything: a funny or witty Christmas message that people will feel compelled to share, or a 4th of July celebration video. The important thing is to make it unique. Make sure it has your logo somewhere at the bottom or at the very end to associate to your brand. If you've been thinking about creating a video to advertise your business, spend the most time on planning. Most people tend to rush through the planning because they are eager to see the end product. And when they see the end product, they aren't as excited. Making a great video means spending a lot of time thinking about the concept and the messaging. What funny or witty messaging can you use to get people's attention? Once you get this part figured out, it becomes easier to create a video that people will really like. Once the video is done, make sure to target the appropriate audiences and channels.

The most successful viral marketing campaigns tend to have an emotional appeal. If your content is filled with love or hate, people won't even think about sharing – it'll happen automatically. You can either be an idiot or a genius with your content or create something that makes people either happy or insanely angry.

Great Landing Pages

If you are a new agent with little online presence at this point, you can focus on landing pages once your online marketing machine gains traction. A landing page is a web page that's designed to specifically cater for a marketing campaign you are running. If you're creating a banner ad, for example, you have limited space to provide information about your products or services. A landing page is placed behind your adverts (on social media, Google, etc.) so that when people click on the ad, they can go to a page with more information. The landing page should be optimized so that it compels people to take the action you want them to.

Do you want them to join your mailing list, preview homes on your website, or view your virtual tours? The landing page helps you convert people, who expressed interest by clicking on your ad, into buyers.

A good real estate landing page should be a continuation of your ad. It should repeat and expand on the message/offer that you presented in the ad. It should also emphasize the benefits of your offer and reinforce your brand identity by using the same colors on your logo and website. Landing pages help make a longer, more targeted pitch so you can make the best out of your advertising.

Here are a few types of landing pages for your real estate business:

a) Home value landing pages
This landing page should focus on helping you grab seller listings leads. Indeed, home value landing pages happen to be the most popular today. How do they work? You create an ad targeting people who are likely to move or sell their home. This ad can be run on Facebook, Google ads, or any other channel where your audience spends time. You want to offer a free home valuation so that people can find out how much their home is worth in the current market. When interested people click on that advert, they end up on your home value landing page.

The title on your home value landing page should be something like *"Find Out How Much Your Home is Worth in Today's Market"*.

Once people convert and provide their information, you can offer an instant valuation or a CMA valuation. An instant valuation needs to be done as soon as people give you their contact information. Thanks to technology, you can use online services such as **Home Value Leads**, **Cloud Attract**, or **Listings to Leads** to get this integrated on your website. A CMA valuation will be done by a professional visiting your lead's home and coming up with a more accurate valuation. It's all up to you whether you want to offer the free valuation or the CMA ones. But users tend to be more open to the instant valuation so you're likely to get a higher conversion rate with that one.

Simple Optimization Tips for Your Online Presence

Real estate agents can no longer ignore search optimization. In many ways, building your website and online presence is like growing a garden. You lay the foundation and plant the seeds, but if you don't nurture the plants, they'll likely die. Studies suggest that real estate related online searches have nearly tripled over the last few years. The majority of homebuyers also search for properties online and you want to position your brand online. Here are a few optimization tips you (or your team) can implement before you're established enough to hire an SEO expert.

a) Keyword research:
Without keyword research, you won't know what *'phrases'* your target audience are using to find real estate agents in your area. There are lots of paid keyword research tools out there, but you can start with the Google Keyword Research Tool (which is free). You may also outsource keyword research to freelancers on Fiverr, Upwork, or other similar sites. Focus on keywords that signal buying intent, selling intent, or research intent. Buyer and seller intent keywords are highly valuable, but don't ignore research intent keywords: these show that a potential lead is just gathering information. These people might turn into customers much later when they are ready.

Once you find keywords that people are using to find real estate agents in your area, the next step is to optimize your content for these keywords. You want to make sure that you are using relevant keywords in your title, and a few times in the body of your webpage. Don't try to stuff your content with keywords as Google will detect this and potentially de-rank your site. Keywords should be naturally used so that they flow with the rest of the content.

Basically, try to be as authentic as possible and Google will value that.

b) Submit your website to directories and citation sites
Submit your real estate website/business to major local directories. You want to increase your visibility on the **World Wide Web**, right? Directories can be instrumental. Think about how most customers find businesses nowadays. They use their smartphone to search for restaurants, entertainment spots, nail polish joints, and even real estate agents in the area. Once they do, Google (or other search engines) will offer them results with turn by turn directions for these businesses. Google shows businesses that have been submitted to **My Business** as snapshots with ratings, reviews, contact information, and directions through Google Maps. Users pay more attention to these results and you want to make sure your real estate agent business shows up.

Here are some of the top citation sites where you can add your real estate business:
- Google
- Zillow.com / Trulia.com
- Realtor.com
- Yelp
- Loopnet.com (for commercial deals)
- Homes.com
- Homelight.com

Major key: when you add your website to local directories and citations, it's important that your NAP (Name, Address, and Phone) details are consistent in all the entries so that you don't confuse the search engines.

c) Ask for reviews
Major key: Customer reviews play a major role in local SEO. They convince prospects to try your services and let search engines know that your business is legitimate. Focus on *Zillow, Facebook, and Google for reviews*. Consider sending an email to your most

loyal clients and ask them to visit one if not all of your business pages and leave a review. This will help you generate more inbound calls from leads saying they found you online rather than you always cold calling and hunting for new business.

d) Publish local neighborhood statistics and information
Prospective home sellers and buyers searching for information on a particular neighborhood want to know the median household income, crime rate, schools, and other information. If you don't have a blog on your website, consider starting one. By publishing informative and SEO-friendly content, you'll attract organic search traffic from Google and other search engines. Neighborhood statistics and reports published on your website show search engines that you are a relevant authority in that neighborhood.

e) Optimize your website for mobile searches
More people use their phones to find the resources they're interested in online. Over half of real estate prospects will use a mobile device to find your business. Just because your website looks good on desktop doesn't automatically imply that it's good for mobile, too. Use the Google Mobile Friendliness tool to see if you're offering a good user experience for customers who find your business via mobile. And if not, make sure to make your website mobile-friendly, otherwise you're doomed.

Major Key: Local optimization can be a big boost for your business. If you don't have the time to do this, consider outsourcing the task to members of your team, or freelancers on any of the major outsourcing platforms such as Fiverr or Upwork. The bottom line is to make your website as best placed as possible for a piece of the local search pie.

Paid Advertising

Traditional organic search engine optimization is the best way to increase the reach and visibility of your real estate website, because it pays off long-term. If your website is well optimized and ranks well with keywords that are relevant to your business, then you'll be able to attract a lot of targeted leads. But it takes effort and patience to get there. Optimizing your website to rank on the top pages of the search engines is not a one-day gig. It is a consistent effort over time. You'll need to pursue persistent content optimization, interlinking, and other techniques in order to outcompete other real estate agents who are working for a piece of the same pie. Meanwhile, pay to play (also known as pay per click) advertising will help you attract targeted leads in exchange for a small advertising fee.

Many search engines (Google, Bing, Yahoo, etc.) allow advertisers to pay for exposure on search engine results pages. How does this work? Let's say I want to capture people who are searching for "*listing agent Las Vegas*". If my website already ranked at the top of Google for this keyword, I'd have no problem and I'd attract a lot of leads indeed. But since that is not the case, I can use PPC (Pay Per Click) advertising so that Google shows my website at the very top when people search for this keyword. So, people will still be able to see my website as an ad at the very top. By participating in PPC advertising, you generate targeted traffic to your site and even increase brand awareness to your real estate business.

Chapter 9:

Creating Passive Income is the Key

Hopefully, by now, you've understood what it takes to become a top agent in your market, and you have some tricks and tools to help aid you in becoming that. Remember to keep your eyes on the end road though. What is your long-term real estate goal?

Once you've created a consistent and sustainable business as an agent, what is the next step? How about using all of your accumulated knowledge and resources as a real estate agent to build passive income. I'm talking about investing your own income into your future and what you know best: Real Estate. After all, remember, the real wealth and money is not in helping others buy and sell real estate but owning the land yourself. As one of my mentors, Jay "*Mr. Real Estate*", would say, "*Be the lord of your land.*" You'll be surprised at how many agents in your brokerage office don't even own a piece of real estate. They treat their career as a job and forget to invest into their retirement. For that reason, they end up with stress and empty bank accounts when a market crashes or if, God forbid, something was to happen to their health, and they couldn't sell full-time anymore.

Major Key: Your advantage of being a real estate agent is that your knowledge can be used to help you create a passive income stream for yourself early on. This way, you'll be using your real estate career to earn your daily bread, but also as a part of a long-term strategy to own property and earn passive income for yourself.

Why You Should Be Investing in Real Estate

As you should already be aware, real estate is one of the surest and most powerful ways to accumulate wealth. Real estate has made more millionaires than perhaps any other industry. Often I see many real estate agents put their money in stocks, savings accounts, bonds, ETFs, and money market accounts, but own no real estate of their own. That is just insane to me, especially when the beauty of real estate is that it isn't as volatile as these other options are. The amount of opportunities that you are awarded with because you have a license should be enough of a reason in itself.

Here are some of the best benefits of investing in real estate for passive income.

- **Stability** – real estate is a fairly stable investment. Your investment in real estate is not tied to mutual funds and the stock markets. When the market is doing bad and stocks lose value, real estate values do not automatically fall with it.
- **Inflation protection** – inflation is the enemy of wealth accumulation. It erodes value from money and reduces gains made from monetary investments. The advantage with real estate is that it's protected (to some extent) from inflation. Rental rates tend to increase to compensate for inflation. So, as a landlord, you are able to adjust the rental rates each year. This can be done through certain clauses in the lease, or whenever you find a new tenant.
- **Stable growth** – investments, such as stocks, chain investors to annual yield like prisoners. What you receive at the end of the year is the only gain you get. A bad step would lead to a substantial loss of your money. It's common to see people who have invested in stocks lose up to 50% of their value in no time. It's a high-risk investment. On the other hand, real estate essentially protects you from wild market mood swings. It's not common for homes to lose large percentage drops. As long as you do your research well and negotiate fair prices, real estate offers a significantly high return on your investment with limited risk.

Here are the factors that determine how much returns you get from your real estate investment:

- ☐ **Cash flow** - simply put, this is the income left after paying all expenses such as mortgage, insurance, taxes, utilities, repairs, vacancies, capital expenditures, and any other expenses that affect your bottom dollar. All great investors know, *"you make money when you buy not when you sell."* A well-purchased property will provide you with a solid and positive cash flow. Always do your research and factor in these costs before calculating the final cash flow.
- ☐ **Appreciation** – this is the rate at which the value of property increases. Appreciation is not always guaranteed as it's often determined by external factors. Historically though, real estate has always appreciated at an average rate of 3% in America.
- ☐ **Loan pay-down** – when you purchase a property with a mortgage, your loan balance decreases each month. This means that with time, your tenant will essentially be paying the loan for you, helping you to build wealth automatically. Let's assume, for a moment, that you own a $200,000 property that you funded with a $150,000 mortgage. Let's also assume that this property made $0 in cash flow and never climbed in value. After the 15-year mortgage is paid off, you'll now have a property worth $230,000 (assuming you gained appreciation) that you never actually saved for. In essence, your tenant will have paid it down and helped you build more wealth.
- ☐ **Tax benefits** The U.S. government wants to encourage people to invest in real estate. Various constructs in the tax system are designed to help people buy real estate. From the 1031-exchange to the extra tax write-offs, real estate investors tend to pay significantly less than others. This extra cash could be used to purchase more property or pay off the loan faster.

- ☐ **Leverage** – this is one of the biggest advantages of investing in real estate for passive income. You can control a significantly large amount of real estate with a relatively low amount of money. For example, you could acquire a property worth $100,000 with a down payment of 20% ($20,000). Let's assume that the value of the property goes up 10% in a year. You'll now have an investment that's worth $110,000 and you'll already have recouped half of the money you spent for the down payment. Also, this calculation doesn't even factor in the build-up of equity from the decreasing mortgage principal, the cash flow and tax advantage.
- ☐ **Financing** – if you are looking to buy stocks, bonds or mutual funds, you'll need to have the entire sum of money required in your pocket. But when it comes to real estate investment, it's much easier to get financing. Lenders typically loan up to 80% of the market value of a property. In some cases, it is possible to secure up to 90% financing.
- ☐ **Solid asset** – real estate is considered to be one of the greatest assets anyone can own. Even the richest people – the likes of Bill Gates and President Trump – invest a lot in real estate. An investment in property makes for solid collateral, shows strength on the balance sheet, and can be financed much easier compared to many other assets.
- ☐ **Freedom** – investing in real estate doesn't tie you up. It's even easier when you are an agent and you can simply spot great investment opportunities in the course of your day job. Once you acquire property, you'll need to spend a little bit of time on management and record keeping each month. But that's a relief compared to other investments where you have to follow up almost daily.

It's easy to see why so many people choose real estate as their vehicle to accumulate long-term wealth. You've likely read discouraging stories from people who invested in real estate and made losses. In the past, people who have bought in overbuilt neighborhoods – where the supply exceeds demand – have not succeeded at real estate investment. But smart investors know to invest where demand far outstrips supply. If you apply your accumulated knowledge dealing in property to invest in your own, it's highly unlikely that you'd go wrong.

Choosing Your Market Right

Many beginner real estate investors make the mistake of buying property with little to no knowledge of the neighborhood the property is in. If you buy in the wrong neighborhood, you'll be inheriting the problems associated with that location. Your only way out might be to sell the property at a loss.

Savvy real estate investors spend enough time analyzing the neighborhood before they sign any document to buy real estate. The overall health of the market, as well as its future prospects, are two very important considerations.

There are three basic types of real estate markets – *cyclical, linear*, and *hybrid*.

☐ **Cyclical markets** – these are real estate markets characterized by large price move ups and move downs over the years. Property values go up and down like a roller coaster ride. The length of each cycle will vary from one market to the other, but often lasts between 7 and 10 years. Cyclical real estate markets are very common along the east and west coasts of the United States. Household incomes tend to be higher in these markets and land for new construction is in short supply. Good examples of these markets are some locations in *California, New York, New Jersey* and parts of *Florida*. When conditions are right, annual housing price gains in these areas can go up to 30%. However, the local boom tends to burn itself out when prices are pushed up to unaffordable levels. When the '*bubble*' bursts, these markets come '*crashing*' down –

usually due to changes in the economy – bringing property prices down as quickly as they went up.

☐ **Linear markets** – these are typical real estate markets that tend to have a 'flatter' growth curve over time. Price inclines are usually smooth and there are no major spikes and declines in the growth curve. It's very hard for booms and busts to happen in a linear market. These markets are characterized by much lower annual appreciation rates. For that reason, some people will refer to them as '*boring*'. Linear markets tend to offer some of the best capitalization rates and cash-on-cash returns. This is the type of market that's very common in the interior Middle-American heartland (Midwest) as well as some of the southern (*Texas*) and south-eastern states (such as *Georgia, Tennessee,* etc.).

☐ **Hybrid real estate markets** – hybrid markets tend to combine the characteristics of both cyclical and linear. There are periods of slow-growth characteristics, followed by instances of moderate cyclical-style appreciation. *Phoenix, Las Vegas, Seattle, Chicago, Minneapolis-St. Paul* and *Detroit* are some of the real estate markets in this category.

Local Factors to Consider When Choosing a Market

☐ **Employment trends** – employment is a major economic factor that relates to the health of the real estate market. People who are employed have the income to purchase or rent property. On the other hand, people who have no income will have a hard time affording the rent. Make sure you study the employment trends when evaluating neighborhoods in which to invest in real estate. The U.S. Bureau of Labor Statistics (BLS) and the local chamber of commerce are good places to start looking for information on local employment trends.

☐ **Net migration** – this is another major factor that will help you choose the right location for investing in real estate.

What's the rampant migration trend? Are people moving into the market, or out? Demand for housing tends to increase based on the total population in a specific market. If data from Federal and State authorities shows that the population in a certain town is experiencing a consistent upward trend, then you can be sure that property prices will go up in the future as demand for local housing increases. You basically want to study this data so you can position your investment on the right side of the trend.

☐ **Industrial diversification** – markets with a diversified range of industries tend to offer some insulation from market volatility during recessions and harder economic times. Markets that are driven by one or two industries are hit harder and usually take longer before they can fully recover. Real estate investors can mitigate their market risk by focusing on markets that have a broader employment base.

☐ **Schools** – availability of schools in a neighborhood is very important when it comes to residential real estate. Many investors put a lot of emphasis on the ratings of schools. But with regards to buying for investment, having multiple schools located in the area is more important than having top rated schools. Homes in areas where some of the best schools in the district are located often attract very premium pricing compared to the income they generate. Don't assume that renters will be willing to pay premium rents for premium schools.

☐ **Crime** – moderate and middle-income neighborhoods tend to have lower crime rates compared to low-income neighborhoods. A lower crime rate is a desirable characteristic, but it is not the most important factor when it comes to choosing a neighborhood for purposes of real estate investment.

Housing Market Factors to Put into Consideration

Buyer's or seller's market?

A buyer's market is characterized by supply that's higher than demand. For that reason, there are more people looking for buyers than there are people looking to buy houses. In such a market situation, sellers may be inclined to accept lower prices and provide incentives if they want to sell their property. This is the ideal market situation for buyers because they're often able to get a great deal.

In a seller's market, the conditions are the exact opposite. There are more people looking to buy property than there are people trying to sell. Sellers will often see a number of buyers bidding for their property. This essentially drives prices up and buyers have to spend more to get the home they are interested in. Seller's markets are ideal for sellers because they offer better prices for them.

- **Median price trends** – the median price trend is usually a very good factor to indicate market activity. Rises in median prices usually means that sellers are responding to more sales in their neighborhood, which means the market is getting '*hotter*'. Median price inclines may also suggest that homes on the lower part of the markets are selling fast, leaving higher-priced property in the market. Declines in median prices usually indicates that few homes are selling at the current price levels. Thus, property values in the market are dropping as sellers try to price more aggressively.
- **Average days on market** – how long (in days) does it take to sell a property within its relevant price range in this neighborhood? How long does a $200,000 house stay in the market before it's sold? In some markets, this might be 3 weeks. In others, it might take up to 3 months. The 3 months market is referred to as a soft

market. Sellers are likely to give concessions, drop prices, or even choose to wait longer to find a buyer for their property.

☐ **Market inventory trends** – how many homes are available for sale in the market? Studying market inventory trends helps you get an idea of how much supply is available in the market. Inventory tends to be higher during the spring as real estate activity thaws. There's less inventory in the fall or winter as real estate activity slows down.

Finding Good Investment Deals

Good investment deals – in real estate and elsewhere – are not easily handed on a silver platter. Most of the time, they are created through relationships. They are out there, but you're going to have to scratch to find them. Investing in real estate property is not just a number's game. You need to let everyone you come in contact with know you're looking to find more real estate, whether that be to buy, list, or help a client invest in. Think about it, you come across an old friend and let them know you're looking to acquire real estate regardless of the condition. They instantly think about their aunt who has a home that she's been thinking about selling but doesn't have the money to fix it up. So they will connect you with their aunt and now you have an opportunity to help the aunt solve the problem.

To be a successful real estate investor who succeeds in building long-term passive wealth, you need to leverage your connections. You want to reach out to other agents and stakeholders such as wholesalers in your community so that they deliver the kind of property you are interested in. You'll also need to know when the best time to sell property that you've invested in is. Successful investors usually estimate the fix-up costs and transaction expenses, then decide how much profit they need to make.

Major key: The best way to start investing in real estate is to focus on one geographic area and mine it inside out. The beauty for you is that you should already have a good understanding of where you're going to invest and that's right in your own backyard. This way, it'll be easier for you to learn about the new sites and development being brought into that area.

Keep your eyes and ears open to what's going on in your community, and you'll be able to spot excellent investment opportunities and capitalize on them before others from the outside jump in.

Chapter 10:

The Life of a Small Business Owner

While some real estate agents can make a great deal of money, the median income in 2016 was only $44,000 for real estate agents.

"There is no greater country on Earth for entrepreneurship than America. In every category, from the high-tech world of Silicon Valley, where I live, to University R&D, to countless Main Street small business owners. Americans are taking risks, embracing new ideas, and – most importantly – creating jobs." – Eric Ries (Author - The Lean Startup)

Starting your real estate business can be rewarding. But there are challenges along the way. Getting listings can be the hardest part of the business, and most agents die because they cannot get a steady stream of listings. As a success-focused real estate agent, you must be mentally ready to handle the joy, frustration, hope, and setbacks that come with running a real estate business.

One thing I often see when browsing online is stories about how people start small businesses and seemingly get rich overnight. It goes like *'How I made $1003 in a single day!'*, or *'How you can work 3 hours and be rich with an online business!'* There might be a few small business owners that start out and get this kind of success in no time, but you don't want to import this mentality in your own real estate business because here's the reality on the ground: it takes a lot of work and effort before you can reap the results.

Statistics suggest that 90% of all small businesses fail within their first two years. That's a whopping number. To be a successful entrepreneur in any industry, you need to be in the 10%. Real estate is no different. You've got to do things right and avoid the mistakes that everyone else is making. In my own experience, as a real estate agent who started from zero and built a six-figure income within the first year, there are three key things that can help you be in the 10%: never giving up, don't ignore anything, and be authentic.

First thing you need to do: **effectively manage your commissions and income.**

How you manage your money is a very important aspect that will play a huge role in your net profits as well as sustaining your career as a real estate professional. Since your results and commission of work is based on your long-term efforts, it can be a little difficult to manage your cash flow. This is why most agents see their entire commission check come in from the broker and deposit 100% into their bank account. That's a mistake. I'll tell you right now...you need a knowledgeable REAL ESTATE tax professional along with a proven strategy that works. One thing to keep in mind is that when you receive your commission checks, the taxes have not been taken out yet. That's still on you.

Major key: Net commission is what really matters in real estate. When most agents talk about how much they made the previous year, they're usually referring to gross income. It's not about what you've made but how much you KEEP. What are you keeping after all broker splits, transaction fees, etc.?

Major key: Remember: start by budgeting 30% off the commission check and take that to a different account where it can keep building up (savings). Then the remaining portion will take care of the bills and taxes. If there's an LLC or P.C (you can talk to your tax professional about these), make sure that you are also budgeting for quarterlies. The last thing you want is for the end of the year to come and for you to receive a huge tax bill that you were not prepared for and didn't budget for correctly.

Be persistent and never give up

Running a real estate business means that just like any other small business owner – you're going to deal with challenges every other day. One day you're running to make sure that your real estate business is compliant with your board and broker rules. The next day you're working with an upset client. Challenges will always be there and it's easier to quit. You decided to start your business, so you owe it to yourself not to let anyone or anything stop you from completing your dreams and goals. And don't expect anyone to support you either. You should hold yourself – and only yourself – responsible for how things turn out in the business.

Don't ignore anything

Neil Patel, the founder of Crazy Egg and a few other successful Internet startups, says that entrepreneurs who succeed are often those who '*do not ignore anything*'.

According to Neil, responsibilities overlap in a small business. The founder cannot afford to say things like "*marketing is my assistant's job*", or "*It's my job to lead*". Some of the key factors that lead to the success of a small business are the pesky issues related to the business process, business model, and scalability. Mr. Patel says that small business owners must work *on* their business, not *in* their business. That means they need to be in the heart of the business.

Teresa Boardman's success story also tells us that we cannot ignore anything – especially online marketing. As a real estate agent and broker based in St. Paul, Minnesota, she says that since she started using the Internet to build her business, she has secured write-ups in the Los Angeles Times, Boston Globe, Chicago Tribute, and several real estate publications. She won numerous awards for her St. Paul Real Estate Blog, which attracts between 3,000 and 5,000 visitors weekly. Teresa now speaks at real estate marketing conferences and is often invited to write for other real estate sites beyond her own blog.

"*Most of my business, about 80%, comes from the Internet,*" she says.

Teresa started blogging in November 2005. At that time, most agents were still very skeptical about doing business online. She decided not to ignore the Internet when it was just getting popular as a tool for growth. Thanks to that decision, she got a head start over many of her competitors.

Be who you are (authenticity)

Remember my story about how I got my first clients through open houses? That came from me being true to who I was. I knew getting face to face and displaying my energy would help me land clients sooner. Authenticity and honesty are rule number one, not only in business, but also in life. All small business owners need authenticity and honesty to thrive.

Nobody teaches the importance of authenticity better than the late Apple co-founder, Steve Jobs. During the early days of his company (Apple Inc.), Steve knew the importance of creating '*insanely great*' products. He encouraged his team to create great products, even if this came at the expense of profitability. He knew that even though it would seem like a subtle difference, it would end up meaning everything. Today's leaders and entrepreneurs will do well by staying true to the purpose of their business and by remaining authentic.

Think about it from a real estate perspective. If you are selling a home, think about how you can offer a great, authentic service. Are you being honest with your customers, or are you just focusing on maximizing your profits? Are there any defects or issues your buyer might be concerned about? Is there a reason why you really wouldn't buy this home? If so, let your client know. That's authenticity and honesty.

Great Habits of a Small Business Owner

What makes some people great business owners and others poor business owners? Habits.

Being a strong small business owner is an elusive goal. There's no single recipe or one-size-fits-all formula to achieve this. But developing the right habits can help you succeed in your small business enterprise.

- ☐ **Take care of yourself** – smart business owners know that having a healthy body is key to having a sharp mind. They make conscious efforts to take care of themselves by eating healthy and physically exercising. Others might see this as an overly indulgent behavior but, in essence, it's seen as necessary maintenance for the most critical tool – the brain.
- ☐ **Get a life outside your business too** – we all want to succeed in our business endeavors. But spending too much time engrossed on your business could lead to you hitting mental walls. It's important to lead a balanced life and take a little bit of time for other interests outside of work. This is essential for growth. You'll be able to expose yourself to a diverse range of other stimuli and give your brain the rest it you being honest with your customers, or are you just focusing on maximizing your profits? Are there any defects or issues your buyer might be concerned about? Is there a reason why you really wouldn't buy this home? If so, let your client know. That's authenticity and honesty.

Many people see a lucrative opportunity and jump on it, even at the expense of authenticity. As a result, they usually end up floundering sooner rather than later. On the other hand, successful small businesses owners will wait until they find an opportunity that is right. Where they can use their skills and experience to honestly solve challenges for their clients. needs. In the real estate industry, time spent in other activities could also be time used to make valuable new acquaintances for your business.

- ☐ **Be a pioneer** – some of the best small business owners are pioneers. They think forward even beyond the proven marketing trends. They are strategic and competitive. Instead of just waiting for things to happen and then react to them, they try to figure out how the market might go. They consistently keep their eyes open for new ways of doing things.
- ☐ **Get organized** – being organized is important to staying productive. Being organized means that you have good ideas and you're able to follow through with them. Keeping your meetings, deadlines, and business plan on a highly organized schedule, then sticking to it, creates the framework your small business needs to thrive.
- ☐ **Nurture relationships** – it's easy to get caught up in the day-to-day work and forget to nurture your clients. The importance of staying in touch and maintaining thoughtful interactions with clients cannot be underestimated. Successful business owners know that relationships are important and invest the right time to nurture them.
- ☐ **Cut the fat** – successful small business owners are always evaluating and re-evaluating to see what parts of their business can be better streamlined. They make an effort to keep their processes as efficient as possible. For that reason, they are able to thrive ahead of the competition.

Chapter 11:

Time is our Most Valuable Asset

I once watched a video with Warren Buffet and Bill Gates. In the video, Bill describes Warren's calendar and says he was shocked to see nothing on it for 3-4 days at a time. Warren's response was that he focuses on being productive and making sure his time is well spent since there's no such thing as a "*busy badge.*" Let's face it. Real estate can be a very busy and stressful profession. You'll often find that you have multiple tasks to juggle on a regular basis: preparing marketing pieces, attending team meetings, having lunch with lenders, and showing property to prospective buyers. In the midst of all this, many agents get lost in their '*busyness*'.

Successful agents know that time is an invaluable asset. They make a conscious effort to manage it so they can take charge of their business (as opposed to getting lost in 'busyness'). Effective management of time keeps you organized, productive, and in control of the heart of your business. It'll help you do what matters by maximizing your time to handle the tasks necessary to grow your business. In this brief chapter, I offer my 4 best tips for effective time management in real estate.

Prioritize and organize

The first step to effective time management is identifying priorities. For most agents, that would be lead-generation or other tasks related to prospecting. Identify tasks that are most important to the progress of your business, and prioritize them in the morning. For instance, I put aside two hours every morning for purposes of prospecting. This way, before I go to sleep every night, I know what I'm going to do in the morning. Organizing your day in advance gives you the clarity you need to spend your time productively.

Ready-to-win agents prioritize activities in order of their importance. The most important tasks (e.g. lead generation with a focus on seller listings) have to be done first. Only then will they take on other less important activities. Not-ready-to-win agents are disorganized. They don't have a plan or strategy for being efficient with their time. So, when they wake up, they'll pick the easier tasks first and get them done. Then, at some point in the day, they'll try to handle the *'vegetable tasks'* (tasks that are bigger and require more focus). But by this time, the vegetables are hard, cold, and they're not very easy to stomach. They require more energy at a time when the agent is already worn out.

Budgeting your time will help you allocate the right tasks to the right time. It's hard to manage your time if you don't have a time-budget. What happens when you wake up at…let's say, 7 AM? Do you go for a 30-minute jog? Do you then get to your office and work on lead generation for two hours? That done, do you have appointments next on your schedule? If you don't have a time-plan that answers these questions, you're going to randomize your tasks in the morning – killing productivity and motivation when it should be at its peak. Time budgeting allows you to use your calendar as a powerful tool so you can do the 20% needed to achieve 80% of the results. It's important to have a clear schedule for various tasks. This way, you can set expectations right with clients. You can let them know that you are going to return their missed calls between this and that hour…and that you are going to email them once daily.

Keeping things organized this way helps me keep track and accomplish more in a specific period of time. There are many time management tools (e.g. Evernote.com) that make productivity tracking much easier.

Don't get me wrong, of course we all need a little flexibility to be able to handle the various situations life throws our way. The point is to block out enough time first to be able to handle your crucial tasks. It's all about protecting certain sections of your time, because it's when you're at your most productive stage and your business really needs it. If you consistently nurture your business by giving it the fertilizer and moisture it needs (lead generation, listings, etc.), you'll be surprised at how quickly you'll grow a garden.

Time blocking

Distractions compete for your attention from the moment you wake up till you go to sleep. Trying to be productive in the midst of chaos can be a bigger challenge than most real estate agents would like to admit. To succeed as a real estate agent, you need to block out distractions and commit your time to activities that really count to grow your business. One of the biggest distractions is checking social media sites and replying to email messages or text messages in the midst of a larger activity. Stay offline (if you can) and just learn to say 'No' to your urges when you're engaged in a priority task. Identify problems, situations, and people who distract you. Eliminate these distractions so you can be able to work with focus.

Delegate tasks

When I first started to have more business than I could efficiently keep up with, I did some research on what should be my first hire. Most people in the industry will tell you when a real estate agent gets busy, the first hire should be an assistant to help with contracts, paperwork, and other smaller tasks. After all, being in sales, the thing we love the most should be talking to people and making sales, so where does that leave paperwork? At the bottom! In the beginning, it's very much a necessity to do your own paperwork so you completely understand what's needed and, especially, become knowledgeable on the contracts, but once you are doing a consistent 5 million in volume+ a year, it's time to scale up. It makes great sense to get some help and delegate tasks rather than choke yourself up trying to get everything done. When you have an extra hand to take care of the minor tasks, you can focus your energy on the bigger tasks. It is also important to figure out what your time is worth. If your time is worth $50/hr, and you can get someone else to do the same task just as well at $12/hr, then it makes more sense to hire. Remember this great saying to live by, *"If you don't have an assistant...you are the assistant."*

Avoid time wasters

However good a time management plan you have, it's possible that time wasters will crop up and distract you from the right course. To make the most out of your time, you need to actively watch out for time wasters.

Procrastination is perhaps the most powerful time waster that can distract you from doing what matters. Many agents tend to push the less-than-fun tasks away. If your day's plan has a task that you are not fond of, make sure you do it first. Getting past it will give you a lift and help make the rest of your day a pleasure. Once you are done with the tasks you don't consider your favorite, you'll clear the way so you can look forward to more fun things.

There are many computer-based contact and task management systems available (some of them free of charge) to you. Make sure that you are taking advantage of tools that can help you make good use of time, not drag along with handwritten notes.

Another time waster plan is falling into the trap of non-critical interruptions of your planned activities. You need discipline to execute your plan successfully. If you're working in a cubicle-divided office, it's going to be easy to get distracted by your workmates. People waste a lot of time on meaningless small tasks and office gossip. Let everyone know when you don't want to be distracted. Be polite but firm. If you have to put a sign up, then go right ahead and get it done. If the office doesn't happen to be such a conducive environment for your core tasks, consider getting things done remotely or from home.

Don't let disappointment and negativity ruin your time management plan. We all have setbacks. Maybe that blown deal or the buyer who had a last-minute change of heart. Things like these will happen all the time. But you needn't let them impact your ability to work according to plan. By focusing on the positive – keeping in mind that it's your plan that produces all the great transactions – you'll be able to jump right back after a disappointment.

We all have the same amount of time each and every single day. What we do with that time is entirely up to us. It's common to hear people saying, "*I don't have enough time for this or that*". The most successful agents have the same 24 hours in their day and they are able to do what needs to get done, and still have time left for family and personal engagements. So, whining about not having enough time is just an excuse for not getting things done. Our problems have nothing to do with how much time is in the day. Our problems have to do with our priorities, leveraging, and proper delegation. We tend to structure our schedules around what we feel are priorities already. Is that consistent with what will help our business increase though? Just think about it – what did you do yesterday? Was it what you set out to do? Was it productive? If your spouse or children were to follow you around for an entire day, what would they say about your work ethic? Answer these questions at the end of each week and you'll get a hint of what you're already prioritizing. It's your job to manage your time around all the priorities so that your challenges do not create barriers. Without choosing to prioritize the important tasks that will help you grow your real estate business (e.g. lead generation), your results will be no different. It's just that simple.

Chapter 12:

4x Your Life

Life is all about living your dreams. Most people keep on waiting for the perfect time to start going after big dreams and goals, but the only perfect time is now. Don't worry about the conditions and circumstances, just start. Every great organization – the likes of Apple, Microsoft, and even Keller Williams Realty – started with a single employee. Every great author starts with a single paragraph. Every great athlete starts with winning a local competition. Every great singer starts in front of the mirror. It's time to shake your mind, body, and soul, and sail in the journey of your dreams.

Think big. There's magic in thinking big. Whatever goals you have right now, write them down and 4x them. Act bigger, live bigger. Making big changes in your life and reaching greater heights starts with thinking big. Your thoughts create the circumstances and situations of your life. Keep your mind open to see opportunities and take advantage of them. Again, think bigger and make greater effort. Because that is the only path to true success!

Major key: The primary objective of this book is to give you the inspiration you need to hit the ground running as well as practical and tactical strategies to aid you. As long as you prioritize your time, focus on the tasks that matter for growth, and offer a truly authentic service – you'll be in a position to influence your clients in a positive way and be in control of how successful you want to be as a real estate agent. However, you must understand that while being a real estate agent can be a promising and meaningful career, it's still a job at the end of the day. The goal is to use the income you're bringing in and invest it so you can build wealth and a legacy for your family and have the freedom to work when and how you choose.

Keep in mind that real estate is and always will be a people business. That is first and foremost. With all the marketing tools, organizational innovations, and other resources available to help you attract leads, it's easy to forget what real estate is all about – nurturing relationships while helping people buy and sell homes. Agents who prioritize service qualities and their core values – honesty, efficiency, and a personalized service – will have people lining up. That is the foundation.

Take a long look and be a problem solver. When our country's economy is doing good and the market is hot, many people tend to think that the good times will last forever. The best agents and investors know they couldn't be more wrong. Always remember, what goes up must come down: real estate is no different. It goes in cycles just like our economy. What makes successful agents different is that they don't ride this emotional roller coaster. They prepare for the future by prospecting daily and staying in touch with their sphere of influence and database. No matter where you are in your business, every 3 months, you should take a moment to analyze where the market was, currently is, and where it will be going over the next 6-12 months.

Your success in this industry is influenced by your ability to solve problems. So forget the commission and focus on helping people solve their housing problems. The more problems you can solve, the more money you can make. If you steer your clients to problems that have the biggest financial reward for you, you'll lose your authenticity. People will lose confidence in you and you will also lose respect for yourself.

Don't sell yourself short. It's disappointing when an agent who has tremendous potential thinks that they can only make modest achievements. If you let this kind of ceiling sit above your head, then you'll only be able to achieve that much. To succeed as a real estate agent means you have to be aware of what's truly possible in your mind. You've got to change your mindset to open the doors for the millionaire real estate agent potential lurking within you. Even the most successful real estate agents in this country had to start from somewhere. A rare few are gifted. But most of them are simply people of average abilities who were determined to dream the big dream.

Conclusion

Thank you again for purchasing this book!

Hopefully, if you didn't before, you now have a strong understanding and realize that your mindset, discipline, and openness to innovation will determine your success in real estate. It doesn't matter what your background is, who you know, or how much money you have,

"when you want to succeed as bad as you want to breathe, then you'll be successful".

Shout out to my guy, Eric Thomas, for that one ;).

So, what are you waiting for? Imagine and create big goals, believe in yourself, seek the education, and take action! This book was intended to equip you with all the fundamentals you need to build relationships, market yourself more effectively, and make great things happen wherever you are in your real estate career. It's all up to you now. Are you going to take action or not?

Without you taking action, this book or any other for that matter will only be pieces of information. So, think about what you want to achieve as a real estate agent and start taking action - today!

Finally, if you enjoyed this book, then I'd like to ask you for a favor: would you be kind enough to leave a review for this book on Amazon? It'd be greatly appreciated!

Click here to leave a review for this book on Amazon!

Thank you for reading my story and good luck!

Made in the USA
Columbia, SC
14 March 2019